# ORIGO
# STEPPING STONES
## 2.0
### COMPREHENSIVE MATHEMATICS

**AUTHORS**

James Burnett

Calvin Irons

Peter Stowasser

Allan Turton

**PROGRAM CONSULTANTS**

Diana Lambdin

Frank Lester, Jr.

Kit Norris

**CONTRIBUTING WRITERS**

Debi DePaul

Beth Lewis

**STUDENT BOOK B**

ORIGO
EDUCATION

# CONTENTS

© ORIGO Education

# CONTENTS

© ORIGO Education

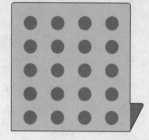

**Step In** · **What do you know about this array?**

How can you figure out the total number of dots?

Write a multiplication fact to describe the array.

**What do you know about this array?**

How could you use the first array to figure out
the total number of dots in this array?

The first array shows 5 rows of 4.
That's 20 so 6 rows of 4 is 4 more.
That's 24.

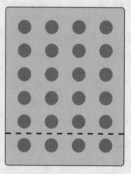

Write two multiplication facts to describe the second array.

**What other facts involving 6 could you solve using this strategy?**

**Step Up** · I. Look at these arrays. Complete the sentences.

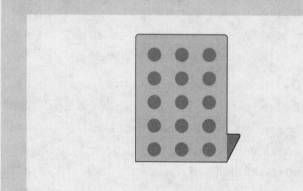

SO

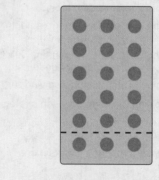

5 rows of 3 = _____

6 rows of 3 = _____

**2.** Write the product for the fives fact. Then use that fact to help you complete the sixes fact and its turnaround.

**a.**

$5 \times 7 =$ _____

SO

___ × ___ = ___

___ × ___ = ___

**b.**

$5 \times 6 =$ _____

SO

___ × ___ = ___

___ × ___ = ___

**c.**

$5 \times 8 =$ _____

SO

___ × ___ = ___

___ × ___ = ___

**3.** Use the same strategy to complete these.

**a.**

$5 \times 9 =$ _____

SO

___ × ___ = ___

___ × ___ = ___

**b.**

$5 \times 2 =$ _____

SO

___ × ___ = ___

___ × ___ = ___

**c.**

$5 \times 5 =$ _____

SO

___ × ___ = ___

___ × ___ = ___

**Step Ahead** Figure out each mystery mass.

 weighs 6 lb

**a.**

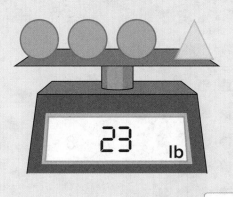

23 lb

 weighs _____ lb

**b.**

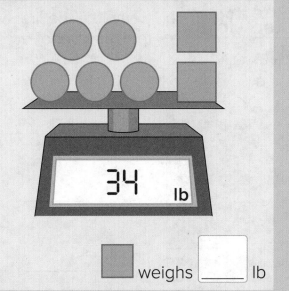

34 lb

weighs _____ lb

**Step In**

What multiplication fact does this whole array show?

How could you figure out the total number of dots?

Complete these facts to help you.

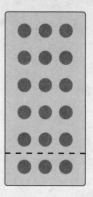

$5 \times 3 =$ _____

$1 \times 3 =$ _____

There are 18 dots in total because 15 + 3 is 18.

What multiplication fact does this whole array show?

What fives fact can you use to help figure out the total number of dots?

Write a multiplication fact to match the array.
Then write the turnaround fact.

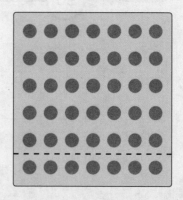

_____ $\times$ _____ = _____

_____ $\times$ _____ = _____

**Step Up**

1. Complete the first two multiplication facts to help you calculate the total number of dots. Then complete the sixes fact.

a.

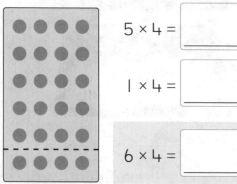

$5 \times 4 =$ _____

$1 \times 4 =$ _____

$6 \times 4 =$ _____

b.

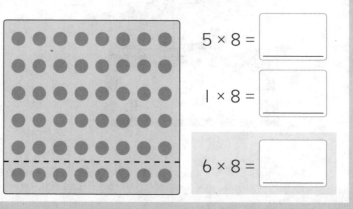

$5 \times 8 =$ _____

$1 \times 8 =$ _____

$6 \times 8 =$ _____

**2.** Complete each of these.

**a.**

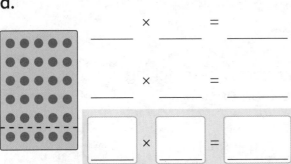

_____ × _____ = _____

_____ × _____ = _____

☐ × ☐ = ☐

**b.**

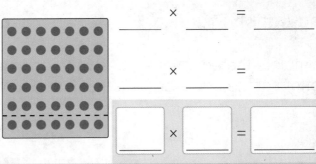

_____ × _____ = _____

_____ × _____ = _____

☐ × ☐ = ☐

**3.** Color the ◯ beside the thinking you could use to calculate the product in the sixes fact. Then write the product.

**a.**
$6 × 6 =$ ☐

◯ 5 × 6 then add 1 × 6

◯ 5 × 7 then add 1 × 7

◯ 6 × 5 then add 1 × 5

**b.**
$6 × 2 =$ ☐

◯ 2 × 5 then add 1 × 5

◯ 5 × 6 then add 1 × 2

◯ 5 × 2 then add 1 × 2

**c.**
$6 × 9 =$ ☐

◯ 5 × 5 then add 1 × 5

◯ 5 × 9 then add 1 × 9

◯ 1 × 6 then add 1 × 9

**Step Ahead**

**a.** Write numbers to continue the pattern.

**b.** Write what you notice.

_____

_____

_____

_____

_____

_____

_____

6 = 5 × 1 + 1

12 = 5 × 2 + 2

18 = ___ × ___ + ___

24 = ___ × ___ + ___

30 = ___ × ___ + ___

36 = ___ × ___ + ___

42 = ___ × ___ + ___

48 = ___ × ___ + ___

54 = ___ × ___ + ___

60 = ___ × ___ + ___

## Computation Practice

★ Complete the equations. Then write each letter above its matching product at the bottom of the page. Some letters appear more than once.

2 × 6 = ☐ **e**          4 × 8 = ☐ **l**

9 × 5 = ☐ **r**          8 × 9 = ☐ **n**

5 × 5 = ☐ **i**          7 × 4 = ☐ **s**

9 × 4 = ☐ **h**          6 × 8 = ☐ **t**

3 × 8 = ☐ **a**          2 × 8 = ☐ **c**

3 × 5 = ☐ **w**          7 × 8 = ☐ **d**

7 × 5 = ☐ **g**          9 × 2 = ☐ **o**

5 × 6 = ☐ **k**          5 × 4 = ☐ **u**

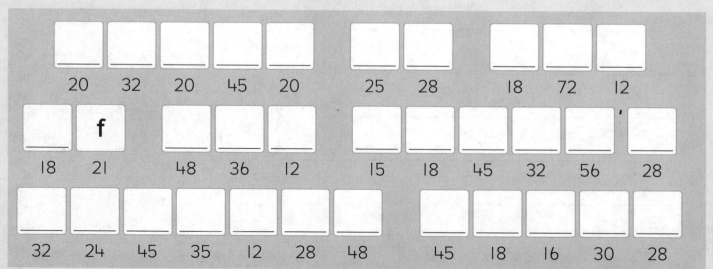

20  32  20  45  20     25  28     18  72  12

☐ **f**     48  36  12     15  18  45  32  56  28

32  24  45  35  12  28  48     45  18  16  30  28

## Ongoing Practice

**1.** Look at the number of whole squares and part squares inside each picture. Write the total number of squares for each.

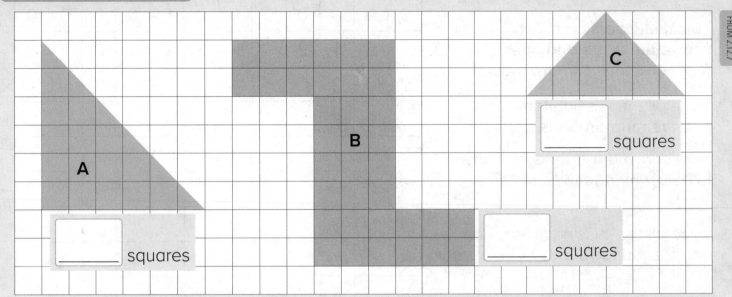

_____ squares

B

C

_____ squares

_____ squares

**2.** Write the product for the fives fact. Then use the fact to complete the sixes fact and its turnaround.

**a.**

$5 \times 8 =$ _____

SO

$6 \times 8 =$ _____

$8 \times 6 =$ _____

**b.**

$5 \times 3 =$ _____

SO

$6 \times 3 =$ _____

_____ $\times 6 =$ _____

**c.**

$5 \times 7 =$ _____

SO

$6 \times 7 =$ _____

_____ $\times 6 =$ _____

## Preparing for Module 8

Write the missing number to complete each fact.

**a.** _____ $\times 9 = 9$

**b.** $9 \times 10 =$ _____

**c.** $45 =$ _____ $\times 9$

**d.** $2 \times$ _____ $= 18$

**e.** $9 \times$ _____ $= 63$

**f.** _____ $\times 9 = 81$

**g.** $4 \times 9 =$ _____

**h.** _____ $\times 9 = 54$

**i.** $27 = 9 \times$ _____

### Step In

This multiplication chart shows the zeros and ones facts and their turnarounds.

Write all the missing tens facts and their turnarounds.

How can you use the tens facts to help write the fives facts?

Write all the missing fives facts and their turnarounds.

Write all the products you could find using a doubling strategy.

What facts do these show?

| × | 0 | 1 | 2 | 3 | 4 | 5 | 6 | 7 | 8 | 9 | 10 |
|---|---|---|---|---|---|---|---|---|---|---|----|
| 0 | 0 | 0 | 0 | 0 | 0 | 0 | 0 | 0 | 0 | 0 | 0 |
| 1 | 0 | 1 | 2 | 3 | 4 | 5 | 6 | 7 | 8 | 9 | 10 |
| 2 | 0 | 2 | | | | | | | | | |
| 3 | 0 | 3 | | | | | | | | | |
| 4 | 0 | 4 | | | | | | | | | |
| 5 | 0 | 5 | | | | | | | | | |
| 6 | 0 | 6 | | | | | | | | | |
| 7 | 0 | 7 | | | | | | | | | |
| 8 | 0 | 8 | | | | | | | | | |
| 9 | 0 | 9 | | | | | | | | | |
| 10 | 0 | 10 | | | | | | | | | |

_____ facts          _____ facts          _____ facts

Write the products of the sixes and nines facts and their turnarounds.

What strategy do you use to figure these out?

**Circle the last four missing products in the chart and write the matching facts below.**

☐ × ☐ = ☐          ☐ × ☐ = ☐

☐ × ☐ = ☐          ☐ × ☐ = ☐

What do you notice about these last facts?

 They all involve a 3 or a 7.

What strategies could you use to calculate the products?

Solve each of these facts involving 3 or 7.
Show the strategy you used.

a.

$8 \times 3 =$ ____

b.

$7 \times 4 =$ ____

c.

$3 \times 9 =$ ____

d.

$9 \times 7 =$ ____

e.

$6 \times 3 =$ ____

f.

$3 \times 7 =$ ____

g.

$3 \times 3 =$ ____

h.

$7 \times 7 =$ ____

**Step Ahead**    Study this fact trail. Each fact can be figured out from $10 \times 3$.

$18 \times 3 \leftarrow 9 \times 3 \leftarrow 10 \times 3 \rightarrow 5 \times 3 \rightarrow 6 \times 3 \begin{array}{c} 3 \times 3 \\ 7 \times 3 \end{array}$

Write your own fact trail that begins with $10 \times 7$.

### Step In

Part of this multiplication chart has been covered.

What are some facts that are hidden?

**David is thinking of a multiplication fact that has a product close to 23.**

What facts could he be thinking about?

6 × 4 has a product that is close.

| × | 0 | 1 | 2 | 3 | 4 | 5 | 6 | 7 | 8 | 9 | 10 |
|---|---|---|---|---|---|---|---|---|---|---|----|
| 0 | 0 | 0 | 0 | 0 | 0 | 0 | 0 | | | | 0 |
| 1 | | | | | | | | | | | 10 |
| 2 | | | | | | | | | | | 20 |
| 3 | | | | | | | | | | | 30 |
| 4 | 0 | | | | | | | | | | 0 |
| 5 | 0 | | | | | 25 | 30 | 35 | 40 | 45 | 50 |
| 6 | 0 | 6 | 12 | 18 | 24 | 30 | 36 | 42 | 48 | 54 | 60 |
| 7 | 0 | 7 | 14 | 21 | 28 | 35 | 42 | 49 | 56 | 63 | 70 |
| 8 | 0 | 8 | 16 | 24 | 32 | 40 | 48 | 56 | 64 | 72 | 80 |
| 9 | 0 | 9 | 18 | 27 | 36 | 45 | 54 | 63 | 72 | 81 | 90 |
| 10 | 0 | 10 | 20 | 30 | 40 | 50 | 60 | 70 | 80 | 90 | 100 |

**Nancy is thinking of a multiplication fact that has a product greater than 70 but less than 80.**

What facts could she be thinking about?

How could you use the multiplication chart to help your thinking?

### Step Up

1. Write four multiplication facts to match each of these.

**a.** Facts with a product close to 39

**b.** Facts with a product close to 52

**c.** Facts with a product close to 46

**d.** Facts with a product close to 11

**2.** Write three multiplication facts to match each of these.

**a.** Facts with a product greater than 40 but less than 50

**b.** Facts with a product greater than 30 but less than 40

**c.** Facts with a product greater than 20 but less than 30

**d.** Facts with a product greater than 35 but less than 45

**Step Ahead**

Figure out the mystery fact. Write clues for a different mystery fact. Then exchange your puzzle with another student to find the solution.

**MYSTERY FACT**

**Clue 1**
If you add the digits of my product the total is **10**.

**Clue 2**
My mystery fact is a **fours** fact.

The mystery fact is:

_____ × _____ = _____

**YOUR MYSTERY FACT**

**Clue 1**
If you add the digits of my product

the total is _____ .

**Clue 2**
My mystery fact is a _____ fact.

The mystery fact is:

_____ × _____ = _____

**Think and Solve**  Look at the equation.

△ − 3 = 6 + ◯

a. If ◯ is 10, what is △? ☐

b. If ◯ is 14, what is △? ☐

c. What are some other numbers for ◯ and △ that make the equation true?

**Words at Work**   Write about two different strategies you could use to solve this equation.

$7 \times 7 = ?$

## Ongoing Practice

1. Use your ruler to draw equal rows and columns of squares. Then write the total number of squares in each rectangle.

**a.**

_____ squares

**b.**

_____ squares

2. Complete the first two multiplication facts to help you figure out the total number of dots. Then complete the sixes fact.

**a.**

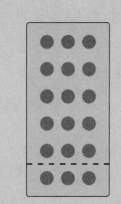

$5 \times 3 =$ _____

$1 \times 3 =$ _____

$6 \times 3 =$ _____

**b.**

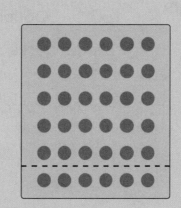

$5 \times 6 =$ _____

$1 \times 6 =$ _____

$6 \times 6 =$ _____

## Preparing for Module 8

Write the product for the fives facts. Then use that fact to help you complete the sixes facts and its turnaround.

**a.**

$5 \times 9 =$ _____

**SO**

$6 \times 9 =$ _____

$9 \times 6 =$ _____

**b.**

$5 \times 8 =$ _____

**SO**

$6 \times 8 =$ _____

__ $\times 6 =$ _____

**c.**

$5 \times 4 =$ _____

**SO**

$6 \times 4 =$ _____

__ $\times 6 =$ _____

$5
BATTERY PACK

$9
BATTERY PACK

**Step In**

Manuel is buying batteries for some toys.
Which pack of batteries is the better value?

It would cost $10 to buy two of the smaller packs of batteries.

He decides to buy 3 large packs of batteries and 1 small pack.

How many batteries did he buy?
What is the total amount that he should pay?

I'll call the total amount **A**. A = 3 × 9 plus 5.

**Helen has to buy 10 new batteries. She lists some of the different options.**

Calculate each total cost. Then circle the batteries that she should buy.

| Option A | Option B | Option C |
| --- | --- | --- |
| 3 small packs | 2 large packs | 1 large pack<br>1 small pack |
| _____ batteries in total | _____ batteries in total | _____ batteries in total |
| $_____ | $_____ | $_____ |

**Step Up**

1. Use the battery prices at the top of the page for these problems. Show your thinking.

a. Hannah has a $20 bill and a $10 bill. She buys 2 large packs of batteries. How much money does she have left in her purse?

$_____

b. Mika spends $19 on batteries. He buys one large pack and some small packs. How many small packs of batteries did he buy?

_____ packs

**2.** Solve each problem. Show your thinking.

**a.** A marching band is standing in 7 rows and 6 columns. 2 more rows of people join them. How many people are in the band now?

_____ people

**b.** Deon needs to cut 7-foot lengths of wire. There are 80 feet of wire in total. How many pieces can he cut?

_____ pieces

**c.** One pack of cards is $3. Megan buys some cards with a $20 bill. She gets $5 in change. How many packs of cards did she buy?

_____ packs

**d.** Two friends sell tickets for $5 each. Hunter sells 7 tickets and Andrea sells 12. How much more money has Andrea collected?

$_____

**Step Ahead**

Figure out the total number of oranges in this stack. Each layer of oranges forms the shape of a square. For example, the bottom layer shows 4 rows of 4 oranges. The next layer shows 3 rows of 3 oranges and so on.

There are _____ oranges.

## Step In

**Imagine you had two $50 bills in your wallet.**

Could you buy both of these games? How do you know?

How could you estimate the total cost of the two games?

Monique adds the digits in the tens place first. If the total is close to $100 she adds the digits in the ones place.

Why does she add the digits in the tens place first?

Carter rounded one of the prices to a nearby ten, then added the second price.

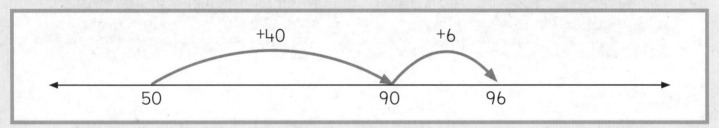

Carter rounds one amount up to a nearby ten and still has enough money to buy both games. With money, it is useful to round up, not down.

**How would you estimate the total of these two prices?**

 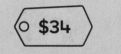

## Step Up

1. Round one number to make it easier to add. Then estimate the sum. Draw jumps on the number line to show your thinking.

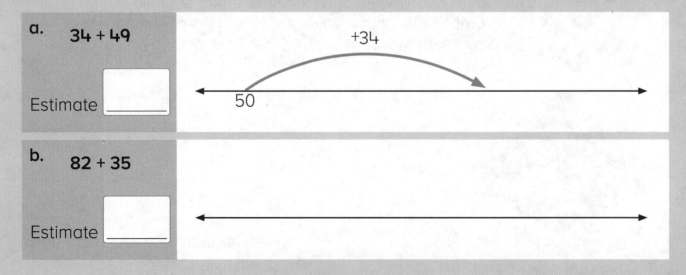

a. **34 + 49**

Estimate _____

b. **82 + 35**

Estimate _____

Use this table to answer Questions 2 and 3, and Step Ahead.

| Tickets Sold | | | | | |
|---|---|---|---|---|---|
| | **Monday** | **Tuesday** | **Wednesday** | **Thursday** | **Friday** |
| **Grade 3** | 45 | 36 | 74 | 39 | 47 |
| **Grade 4** | 29 | 78 | 28 | 65 | 68 |

2. Estimate the total number of tickets sold on each of these days. Then draw jumps on the number line to show how you formed your estimate.

a. **Monday**

Estimate _____

b. **Wednesday**

Estimate _____

c. **Thursday**

Estimate _____

3. Estimate the total number of tickets that were sold by each grade.

a. **Grade 3**

_____

b. **Grade 4**

_____

**Step Ahead**

On Thursday, Grade 5 sold about 50 more tickets than the total number of tickets sold by Grades 3 and 4 combined on that day. Estimate how many tickets Grade 5 sold on Thursday.

_____ tickets

## Computation Practice

★ For each of these, write the multiplication fact you would use to help figure out the division fact. Then write the answers. Use the classroom clock to time yourself.

**Time Taken:**

**start**

$18 \div 2 =$ ___

___ $\times$ ___ $=$ ___

$16 \div 2 =$ ___

___ $\times$ ___ $=$ ___

$36 \div 4 =$ ___

___ $\times$ ___ $=$ ___

$20 \div 2 =$ ___

___ $\times$ ___ $=$ ___

$12 \div 4 =$ ___

___ $\times$ ___ $=$ ___

$28 \div 4 =$ ___

___ $\times$ ___ $=$ ___

$6 \div 2 =$ ___

___ $\times$ ___ $=$ ___

$20 \div 4 =$ ___

___ $\times$ ___ $=$ ___

$12 \div 2 =$ ___

___ $\times$ ___ $=$ ___

$32 \div 4 =$ ___

___ $\times$ ___ $=$ ___

$14 \div 2 =$ ___

___ $\times$ ___ $=$ ___

$16 \div 4 =$ ___

___ $\times$ ___ $=$ ___

$10 \div 2 =$ ___

___ $\times$ ___ $=$ ___

$24 \div 4 =$ ___

___ $\times$ ___ $=$ ___

**finish**

$8 \div 4 =$ ___

___ $\times$ ___ $=$ ___

$8 \div 2 =$ ___

___ $\times$ ___ $=$ ___

## Ongoing Practice

**1.** Write the total number of squares each rectangle covers.

A

B

C

_____ squares

_____ squares

_____ squares

**2.** Write four multiplication facts to match each of these.

**a.** Facts with a product greater than 25 but less than 35.

_____ × _____ = _____

_____ × _____ = _____

_____ × _____ = _____

_____ × _____ = _____

**b.** Facts with a product between 40 and 50.

_____ × _____ = _____

_____ × _____ = _____

_____ × _____ = _____

_____ × _____ = _____

**c.** Facts with a product close to 13.

_____ × _____ = _____

_____ × _____ = _____

_____ × _____ = _____

_____ × _____ = _____

## Preparing for Module 8

Complete the equations to match the jumps on the number line.

**a.**

_____ + _____ + _____ = $\frac{}{5}$

**b.**

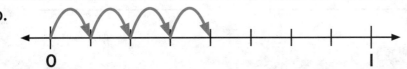

_____ = _____

## Step In

How would you estimate the total cost of these two gifts?

$235

$152

How could you calculate the exact cost?

Look at how these students figured it out.

| Ramon | Karen |
|---|---|
| 235 | 235 |
| + 152 | + 152 |
| 300 | 7 |
| 80 | 80 |
| + 7 | + 300 |
| $387 | $387 |

What did they do the same? What did they do differently?

An algorithm is a set of steps you can use to solve a problem. You could use this standard algorithm to add the prices.

| First you add the ones. | Then you add the tens. | Then you add the hundreds. |
|---|---|---|
| 235 | 235 | 235 |
| + 152 | + 152 | + 152 |
| 7 | 87 | 387 |

Do you think this is an easy way to calculate the total? Why?

## Step Up

1. Estimate the total cost. Then use the standard addition algorithm to calculate the exact cost.

**a.**  $25   $253

Estimate  $_____

| H | T | O |
|---|---|---|
| 2 | 5 | 3 |
| + | 2 | 5 |

**b.**  $413   $135

Estimate  $_____

| H | T | O |
|---|---|---|
| 4 | 1 | 3 |
| + 1 | 3 | 5 |

**c.**  $212   $374

Estimate  $_____

| H | T | O |
|---|---|---|
| 3 | 7 | 4 |
| + |  |  |

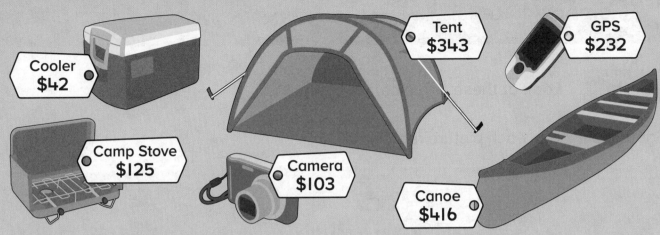

Cooler $42

Camp Stove $125

Tent $343

GPS $232

Camera $103

Canoe $416

**2.** Estimate the total cost of each pair of items in your head. Then use the standard algorithm to calculate the exact cost.

**a.** GPS and Camp Stove.

| H | T | O |
|---|---|---|
| 2 | 3 | 2 |
| + 1 | 2 | 5 |

**b.** Canoe and Camera

| H | T | O |
|---|---|---|
| + | | |

**c.** Tent and GPS

| H | T | O |
|---|---|---|
| + | | |

**d.** Camp Stove and Cooler

| | | |
|---|---|---|
| + | | |

**e.** Tent and Cooler

| | | |
|---|---|---|
| + | | |

**f.** Camera and GPS

| | | |
|---|---|---|
| + | | |

**Step Ahead**

Estimate the total cost. Then use the standard algorithm to calculate the exact cost.

Estimate $_____     Exact cost $_____

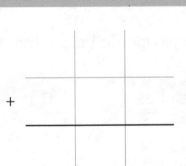

Tamborine $32

Guitar $127

Keyboard $230

© ORIGO Education

**Step In** Look at these two pictures of blocks.

What number does each picture represent?

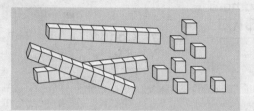 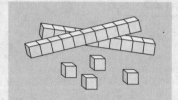

**Imagine you added the blocks together.**

What would be the total?

What is another way to show the same value?

You could regroup 10 ones blocks as 1 tens block.

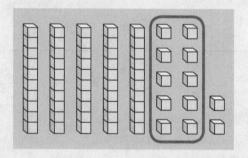 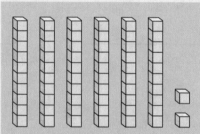

Follow these steps of the standard addition algorithm to add the two stacks of blocks.

| First add the ones. | Then add the tens. |
|---|---|

| H | T | O |
|---|---|---|
|   | I |   |
|   | 3 | 8 |
| + | 2 | 4 |
|   |   | 2 |

| H | T | O |
|---|---|---|
|   | I |   |
|   | 3 | 8 |
| + | 2 | 4 |
|   | 6 | 2 |

What does the number above the 3 represent?

How do you know?

© ORIGO Education

## Step Up

Estimate the total. Then use the standard algorithm to calculate the exact sum.

**a.**

| H | T | O |
|---|---|---|
|   | 5 | 5 |
| + |   | 7 |

**b.**

| H | T | O |
|---|---|---|
|   | 7 | 8 |
| + |   | 9 |

**c.**

| H | T | O |
|---|---|---|
|   | 3 | 9 |
| + |   | 8 |

**d.**

| 2 | 2 | 6 |
|---|---|---|
| + |   | 5 |

**e.**

| 7 | 4 | 4 |
|---|---|---|
| + |   | 9 |

**f.**

| 4 | 8 | 6 |
|---|---|---|
| + |   | 7 |

**g.**

| 6 | 8 |
|---|---|
| + | 1 | 4 |

**h.**

| 5 | 9 |
|---|---|
| + | 2 | 9 |

**i.**

| 4 | 3 |
|---|---|
| + | 3 | 8 |

**j.**

| 3 | 6 | 8 |
|---|---|---|
| + | 1 | 7 |

**k.**

| 6 | 2 | 3 |
|---|---|---|
| + | 5 | 9 |

**l.**

| 8 | 3 | 9 |
|---|---|---|
| + | 1 | 9 |

## Step Ahead

Estimate the total cost. Then use the standard algorithm to calculate the exact cost.

Estimate $ _____     Exact cost $ _____

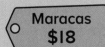

Maracas $18

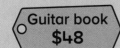

Guitar book $48

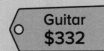

Guitar $332

## Think and Solve  THINK TANK

**a.** Write the names of these girls in order from **shortest** to **tallest**.

- **Last** year, Julia was **shorter** than Shen.
- **This** year Julia is **taller** than Shen.
- Natalie wants to grow as tall as Shen.

**b.** Imagine Shen is 123 cm tall. Write a possible height for Natalie and Julia.

Natalie _____ cm     Julia _____ cm

## Words at Work

Find out where you might estimate to add outside of school. You can talk about it with your family or look it up online. Write about it in words.

## Ongoing Practice

**1.** Write the matching numeral and number name.

**a.**

| 2 | thousands | 0 | 9 | 1 |

_____

**b.**

| 4 | thousands | 1 | 1 | 2 |

_____

**2.** Round one number to the nearest ten. Then estimate the total.
Draw jumps on the number line to show your thinking.

**a.**  69 + 26

Estimate _____

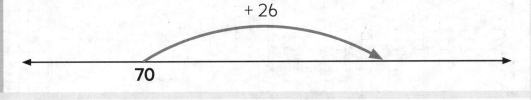

+ 26

70

**b.**  45 + 78

Estimate _____

## Preparing for Module 8

Draw jumps above the number line to match each common fraction.

**a.**

$\frac{4}{5}$

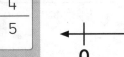

0 ———————————————— 1

**b.**

$\frac{5}{8}$

0 ———————————————— 1

## Step In    Look at these two pictures of blocks.

What number does each picture represent?

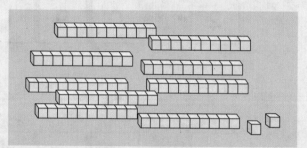

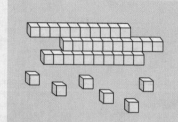

**Imagine you added the blocks together.**

What would be the total?

What is another way to show the same value?

> You could regroup 10 tens blocks as I hundreds block.

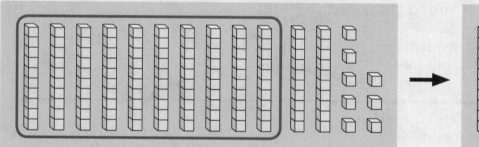

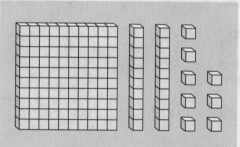

**Follow these steps of the standard addition algorithm to add the two stacks of blocks.**

| First add the ones. | Then add the tens. | Then add the hundreds. |
|---|---|---|

First add the ones.

|   | H | T | O |
|---|---|---|---|
|   |   | 9 | 2 |
| + |   | 3 | 6 |
|   |   |   | 8 |

Then add the tens.

|   | H | T | O |
|---|---|---|---|
|   | I |   |   |
|   |   | 9 | 2 |
| + |   | 3 | 6 |
|   |   | 2 | 8 |

Then add the hundreds.

|   | H | T | O |
|---|---|---|---|
|   | I |   |   |
|   |   | 9 | 2 |
| + |   | 3 | 6 |
|   | 1 | 2 | 8 |

Why is the numeral I written in the hundreds place?

What does it represent?

> 12 tens is equal to I hundred and 2 tens.

Estimate the total. Then use the standard algorithm to calculate the exact sum.

**a.**

| H | T | O |
|---|---|---|
|   | 8 | 2 |
| + | 3 | 4 |

**b.**

| H | T | O |
|---|---|---|
|   | 7 | 6 |
| + | 4 | 3 |

**c.**

| H | T | O |
|---|---|---|
|   | 9 | 1 |
| + | 5 | 3 |

**d.**

| H | T | O |
|---|---|---|
|   | 6 | 8 |
| + | 5 | 1 |

**e.**

| H | T | O |
|---|---|---|
|   | 8 | 3 |
| + | 7 | 4 |

**f.**

| H | T | O |
|---|---|---|
|   | 7 | 4 |
| + | 6 | 0 |

**g.**

| H | T | O |
|---|---|---|
| 2 | 3 | 4 |
| + | 8 | 1 |

**h.**

| H | T | O |
|---|---|---|
| 5 | 4 | 2 |
| + | 9 | 5 |

**i.**

| H | T | O |
|---|---|---|
| 4 | 7 | 3 |
| + | 5 | 5 |

**j.**

| H | T | O |
|---|---|---|
| 7 | 8 | 4 |
| + | 6 | 4 |

**k.**

| H | T | O |
|---|---|---|
| 6 | 2 | 7 |
| + | 9 | 2 |

**l.**

| H | T | O |
|---|---|---|
| 8 | 8 | 2 |
| + | 7 | 6 |

**Step Ahead**

Estimate the total cost. Then use the standard algorithm to calculate the exact cost.

Estimate $_____

Exact cost $_____

Table $83

Desk lamp $21

Chair $473

**Step In**

This table shows the number of people who visited an art gallery over the weekend.

|  | Adults | Children |
|---|---|---|
| Saturday | 273 | 361 |
| Sunday | 192 | 256 |

How could you calculate the total number of people who went on Saturday?

I used the standard algorithm and added the ones first.

$$\begin{array}{r} {\scriptstyle 1} \\ 273 \\ + 361 \\ \hline 634 \end{array}$$

How would you use the standard algorithm to calculate the total number of people who went to the art gallery on Sunday?

What are some other totals you could calculate from the table?

**Step Up**

Use this table to answer Questions 1, 2, and 3.

| Number of People Using Weekend Transportation | | | | | | |
|---|---|---|---|---|---|---|
|  | Train | Bus | Car | Ferry | Walking | Other |
| Saturday | 361 | 429 | 535 | 250 | 361 | 82 |
| Sunday | 577 | 354 | 348 | 196 | 329 | 126 |

1. Estimate the total number of people who use each means of transportation on the weekend. Then use the standard addition algorithm to calculate the exact sum.

a. Train

```
  H T O
+
_____
```

b. Bus

```
  H T O
+
_____
```

c. Car

```
  H T O
+
_____
```

| d. | Ferry | e. | Walking | f. | Other |
|----|-------|----|---------|----|-------|

$+$

$+$

$+$

**2.** Calculate how many people in total traveled by **bus** and **ferry** on each day.

| a. | Saturday | b. | Sunday |
|----|----------|----|--------|

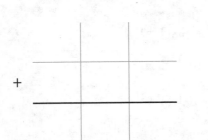

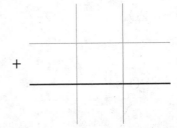

**3.** Calculate how many people in total traveled by **train** and **car** on each day.

| a. | Saturday | b. | Sunday |
|----|----------|----|--------|

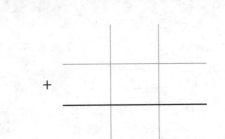

**Step Ahead** Look at the transportation table on page 270. Calculate the total number of people for each of these on Sunday.

**a. Train** and **Bus**

**b. Car** and **Ferry**

## Computation Practice

★ Complete the equations. Then write each letter above its matching difference at the bottom of the page.

550 − 210 = ☐ **m**

640 − 210 = ☐ **d**

470 − 320 = ☐ **a**

780 − 360 = ☐ **n**

380 − 120 = ☐ **h**

860 − 530 = ☐ **e**

690 − 380 = ☐ **r**

560 − 340 = ☐ **t**

760 − 350 = ☐ **p**

460 − 230 = ☐ **o**

870 − 320 = ☐ **w**

980 − 540 = ☐ **s**

580 − 420 = ☐ **b**

360 − 240 = ☐ **i**

Some letters appear more than once.

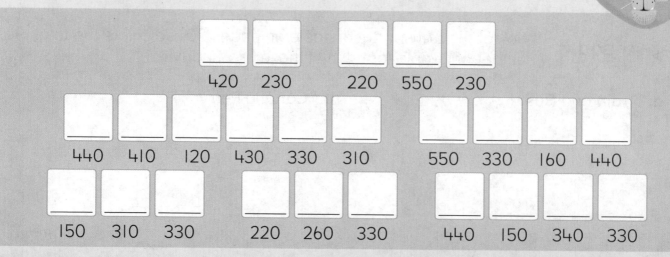

☐ ☐   ☐ ☐ ☐
420 230   220 550 230

☐ ☐ ☐ ☐ ☐ ☐     ☐ ☐ ☐ ☐
440 410 120 430 330 310     550 330 160 440

☐ ☐ ☐     ☐ ☐ ☐     ☐ ☐ ☐ ☐
150 310 330     220 260 330     440 150 340 330

## Ongoing Practice

**1.** Write each numeral in expanded form.

**a.**
6,751

**b.**
4,913

**2.** Estimate the total. Then use the standard addition algorithm to calculate the exact total.

**a.**

Estimate _____

| H | T | O |
|---|---|---|
| 3 | 5 | 6 |
| + | 4 | 2 |

**b.**

Estimate _____

| H | T | O |
|---|---|---|
| 3 | 1 | 5 |
| + 2 | 5 | 4 |

**c.**

Estimate _____

| H | T | O |
|---|---|---|
| 3 | 4 | 2 |
| + 1 | 2 | 4 |

**d.**

Estimate _____

| | | |
|---|---|---|
| 4 | 4 | 8 |
| + 1 | 3 | 1 |

**e.**

Estimate _____

| | | |
|---|---|---|
| 2 | 3 | 4 |
| + 1 | 6 | 2 |

**f.**

Estimate _____

| | | |
|---|---|---|
| 2 | 7 | 5 |
| + 2 | 1 | 3 |

## Preparing for Module 8

For this number line, the distance from 0 to 1 is one whole. Write the fraction that should be in each box.

**a.** **b.** **c.**

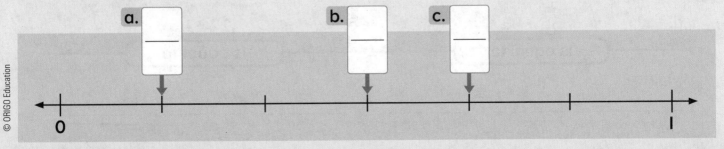

**Step In**

How could you calculate the exact cost of these two items?

$23
$48

Dwane showed each number with base-10 blocks. He then moved the blocks between each group to make it easier to add.

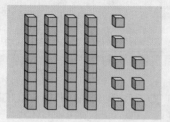 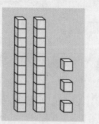  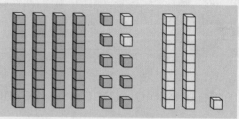

How did the numbers change? Did it affect the total? How do you know?

Dwane then showed his strategy on this number line.

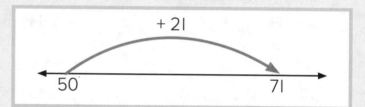

+ 21

50          71

Gloria used a different strategy. She rounded 48 to a nearby ten.

The amount that she added to round (2) is then subtracted afterward to calculate the exact cost.

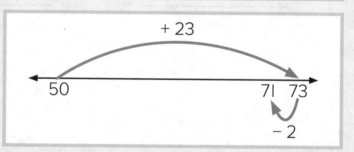

+ 23

50          71  73

− 2

**Step Up**

1. Think about how you can change these numbers to make it easier to add. Then complete the sentence.

a.   **69 + 25**
   is equal to
   70 + _____

b.   **28 + 56**
   is equal to
   30 + _____

c.   **94 + 21**
   is equal to
   _____ + 20

d.   **35 + 98**
   is equal to
   _____ + _____ = _____

e.   **129 + 46**
   is equal to
   _____ + _____ = _____

**2.** Write the sum. Then draw jumps on the number line to show your thinking.

**a.**

$46 + 39 =$ [ ]

⟵————————————————————⟶

**b.**

$19 + 84 =$ [ ]

⟵————————————————————⟶

**c.**

$112 + 44 =$ [ ]

⟵————————————————————⟶

**d.**

$198 + 154 =$ [ ]

⟵————————————————————⟶

**e.**

$279 + 116 =$ [ ]

⟵————————————————————⟶

**Step Ahead**

Try to calculate each total without using the standard addition algorithm. Show your thinking.

**a.**

$59 + 37 =$ [ ]

**b.**

$299 + 56 =$ [ ]

**c.**

$135 + 147 =$ [ ]

**Step In**  What does this table show?

| How Students at Moonby Elementary Go to School | | | | |
|:---:|:---:|:---:|:---:|:---:|
| Bus | Car | Walk | Bike | Other |
| 225 | 197 | 82 | 161 | 30 |

How could you figure out the total number of students who go to school by bus or car?

 Liam used the standard algorithm.

| H | T | O |
|:---:|:---:|:---:|
| \| | \| | |
| 2 | 2 | 5 |
| + 1 | 9 | 7 |
| 4 | 2 | 2 |

Terri used a compensation strategy.

225 + 197 = _____

225 + 200 = 425

425 − 3 = 422

What is the total? How did Terri adjust the numbers to find the answer?

Which strategy do you prefer? Why?

What are some other numbers in the table that you can add?

**Step Up**

1. Use the table at the top of the page to solve each problem. Show your thinking.

a. How many students get to school by walking or riding their bike?

_____ students

b. How many students get to school by bus, bike, or car?

_____ students

**2.** Solve each problem. Show your thinking.

**a.** A letter was sent home to all third grade students. There are 97 girls and 85 boys in Grade 3. How many letters were sent?

_____ letters

**b.** There are 46 fewer students in Grade 2 than Grade 3. There are 125 students in Grade 2. How many students are in Grade 3?

_____ students

**c.** On Monday, 314 students attend a field trip to the museum. On Tuesday, 28 more students attend than on Monday. How many students attend the field trip in total?

_____ students

**d.** The cafeteria sells 420 pints of milk over three days. They sell 119 pints on Monday and 186 pints on Tuesday. How many pints of milk are sold on Wednesday?

_____ pints

**Step Ahead**    Solve this problem. Show your thinking.

Students at Yellow Rock Elementary are organized into 3 sports teams: red, blue, and green. There are 765 students enrolled at the school and the principal likes to make sure that the number of students in each team is similar. How many students might be in each team?

_____ red

_____ blue

_____ green

## Think and Solve

For each square, add the numbers in the **shaded boxes** to figure out the magic number.

Then use the magic number to complete the magic square.

In a magic square, the three numbers in each row, column, and diagonal add to make the same number. This is called the **magic number**.

a.

| 14 | | 16 |
|---|---|---|
| 15 | | 11 |
| 10 | | |

b.

| 21 | | |
|---|---|---|
| | | 22 |
| 25 | | 23 |

## Words at Work

Imagine your friend was away from school when you learned about the standard algorithm for addition. Write the steps that your friend should follow to add 496 and 127.

H  T  O

+
_____

## Ongoing Practice

**1.** Write the number that is shown by each arrow.

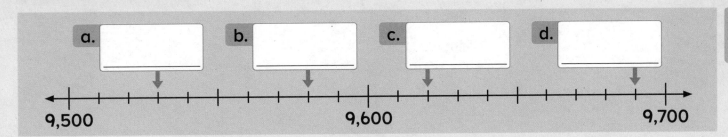

a. [ ]
b. [ ]
c. [ ]
d. [ ]

9,500          9,600          9,700

**2.** Complete these standard addition algorithms.

a.
|  | H | T | O |
|---|---|---|---|
|  | 2 | 5 | 8 |
| + |  | 2 | 7 |
|  |  |  |  |

b.
|  | H | T | O |
|---|---|---|---|
|  | 3 | 1 | 6 |
| + |  | 5 | 7 |
|  |  |  |  |

c.
|  | H | T | O |
|---|---|---|---|
|  | 1 | 4 | 5 |
| + |  | 3 | 8 |
|  |  |  |  |

d.
|  | H | T | O |
|---|---|---|---|
|  | 3 | 2 | 6 |
| + |  | 4 | 5 |
|  |  |  |  |

e.
|  | H | T | O |
|---|---|---|---|
|  | 2 | 1 | 8 |
| + |  | 5 | 6 |
|  |  |  |  |

f.
|  | H | T | O |
|---|---|---|---|
|  | 4 | 5 | 7 |
| + |  | 3 | 8 |
|  |  |  |  |

## Preparing for Module 8

Read the scale. Then write the mass in words.

a.

_____

_____

b.

_____

_____

c.

_____

_____

## Step In

**What are some nines multiplication facts that you know?**

Look at the picture below. What number is covered?

$$9 \times \boxed{\phantom{0}} = 45$$

How do you know?

**What do you know about this array?**

How could you figure out the number of dots in each row?

Write the multiplication fact and division fact that you would use to calculate the number of dots in each row.

$$\boxed{\phantom{0}} \times \boxed{\phantom{0}} = \boxed{\phantom{0}} \qquad \boxed{\phantom{0}} \div \boxed{\phantom{0}} = \boxed{\phantom{0}}$$

27 dots in total

How would you use multiplication to calculate $36 \div 9$?

## Step Up

**I.** Complete the multiplication fact that you would use to figure out the division fact. Then complete the division fact.

**a.**

18 dots in total

$2 \times \underline{\phantom{00}} = 18$

$18 \div 2 = \underline{\phantom{00}}$

**b.**

54 dots in total

$\underline{\phantom{00}} \times 9 = 54$

$54 \div 9 = \underline{\phantom{00}}$

**c.**

36 dots in total

$4 \times \underline{\phantom{00}} = 36$

$36 \div 4 = \underline{\phantom{00}}$

**d.**

90 dots in total

$\underline{\phantom{00}} \times 9 = 90$

$90 \div 9 = \underline{\phantom{00}}$

**2.** Write a multiplication and division fact to match each picture.

**a.**

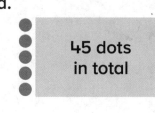 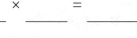 

45 dots
in total

_____ × _____ = _____

_____ ÷ _____ = _____

**b.**

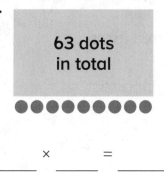

63 dots
in total

_____ × _____ = _____

_____ ÷ _____ = _____

**c.**

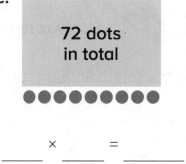 

72 dots
in total

_____ × _____ = _____

_____ ÷ _____ = _____

**d.**

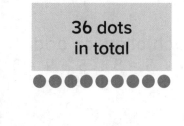

36 dots
in total

_____ × _____ = _____

_____ ÷ _____ = _____

**e.**

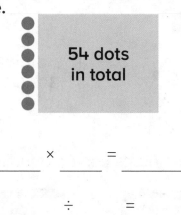

54 dots
in total

_____ × _____ = _____

_____ ÷ _____ = _____

**f.**

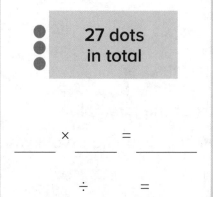

27 dots
in total

_____ × _____ = _____

_____ ÷ _____ = _____

**3.** Write a multiplication and division fact to match this problem.

Drinking glasses are arranged into 9 equal rows. There are 72 glasses in total. How many glasses are in each row?

_____ × _____ = _____

_____ ÷ _____ = _____

**Step Ahead**   Write the missing number in each fact.

**a.** $36 ÷ 9 =$ _____

**b.** $9 = 18 ÷$ _____

**c.** _____ $÷ 9 = 1$

**d.** $9 = 45 ÷$ _____

**e.** _____ $÷ 9 = 9$

**f.** $3 =$ _____ $÷ 9$

**Step In**   Lisa wrote these nines facts.

Circle the multiplication fact that is incorrect.
Then write the correct fact.

| | | | |
|---|---|---|---|
| | × | | = |

$4 \times 9 = 36$

$5 \times 9 = 45$

$6 \times 9 = 54$

$7 \times 9 = 62$

$8 \times 9 = 72$

What do you notice about the
product of each nines fact?

The digits in each product add to 9.
$3 + 6 = 9$   $4 + 5 = 9$   $5 + 4 = 9$

**Look at the jars below.**

How could you figure out which amounts can be equally shared among nine?

81 marbles    53 marbles    60 marbles    27 marbles

**What are some other amounts you know can be equally shared among nine?**

**Step Up**   1. Color one circle to show an amount that can be equally shared
among nine. Then color an array to show how the amount can
be split into equal rows.

a.

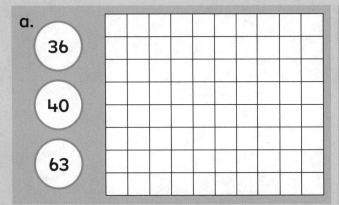

36

40

63

b.

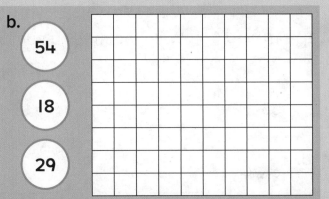

54

18

29

**2.** Color an array to match the numbers given. Then complete the fact family to match.

**a.**

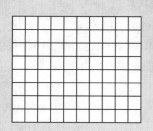

$5 \times 9 =$ _____

_____ $\times$ _____ $=$ _____

_____ $\div$ _____ $=$ _____

_____ $\div$ _____ $=$ _____

**b.**

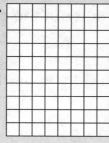

$9 \times 3 =$ _____

_____ $\times$ _____ $=$ _____

_____ $\div$ _____ $=$ _____

_____ $\div$ _____ $=$ _____

**c.**

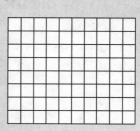

$1 \times 9 =$ _____

_____ $\times$ _____ $=$ _____

_____ $\div$ _____ $=$ _____

_____ $\div$ _____ $=$ _____

**d.**

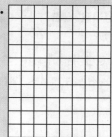

$9 \times 6 =$ _____

_____ $\times$ _____ $=$ _____

_____ $\div$ _____ $=$ _____

_____ $\div$ _____ $=$ _____

**3.** Complete each equation. Then use the same color to show the number facts that belong in the same fact family.

| | | | |
|---|---|---|---|
| $72 \div 9 =$ _____ | $10 =$ _____ $\div 9$ | $9 \times 5 =$ _____ | _____ $= 36 \div 9$ |
| _____ $= 10 \times 9$ | $45 \div 5 =$ _____ | _____ $= 8 \times 9$ | $9 \times 5 =$ _____ |
| _____ $\div 4 = 9$ | $45 =$ _____ $\times 9$ | _____ $\div 8 = 9$ | _____ $= 4 \times 9$ |

**Step Ahead**    Circle an amount that you think can be equally shared among nine. Then calculate the answer to check your prediction.

100 marbles    119 marbles    190 marbles    108 marbles

**Computation Practice**    **Why did the tiger spit out the clown?**

★ For each of these, write the product and the turnaround fact. Then write each letter above its matching product in the grid. Some letters appear more than once.

$8 \times 1 = $ ___ = ___ × ___  **t**        $10 \times 8 = $ ___ = ___ × ___  **u**

$6 \times 8 = $ ___ = ___ × ___  **h**        $8 \times 4 = $ ___ = ___ × ___  **y**

$8 \times 3 = $ ___ = ___ × ___  **e**        $9 \times 8 = $ ___ = ___ × ___  **a**

$8 \times 5 = $ ___ = ___ × ___  **n**        $8 \times 7 = $ ___ = ___ × ___  **s**

$8 \times 8 = $ ___ = ___ × ___  **d**        $2 \times 8 = $ ___ = ___ × ___  **f**

| | | | | | | | |
|---|---|---|---|---|---|---|---|
| 48 | 24 | | 8 | 72 | 56 | 8 | 24 | 64 |

| | | | | |
|---|---|---|---|---|
| 16 | 80 | 40 | 40 | 32 |

Complete these facts as fast as you can.

$5 \times 6 = $ ___        $8 \times 6 = $ ___        $1 \times 6 = $ ___

$6 \times 2 = $ ___        $6 \times 9 = $ ___        $6 \times 6 = $ ___

$4 \times 6 = $ ___        $7 \times 6 = $ ___        $3 \times 6 = $ ___

1. Complete these standard addition algorithms.

a.
| H | T | O |
|---|---|---|
| 6 | 3 | 1 |
| + | 8 | 7 |
|   |   |   |

b.
| H | T | O |
|---|---|---|
| 2 | 5 | 6 |
| + | 7 | 3 |
|   |   |   |

c.
| H | T | O |
|---|---|---|
| 4 | 6 | 7 |
| + | 5 | 2 |
|   |   |   |

d.
| | 3 | 8 | 0 |
|---|---|---|---|
| + | | 4 | 7 |
| | | | |

e.
| | 2 | 4 | 0 |
|---|---|---|---|
| + | | 6 | 8 |
| | | | |

f.
| | 4 | 5 | 7 |
|---|---|---|---|
| + | 1 | 7 | 0 |
| | | | |

g.
| | 5 | 6 | 3 |
|---|---|---|---|
| + | 2 | 5 | 5 |
| | | | |

2. Complete facts to match each of these.

a.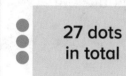
27 dots in total

× _____ = _____

÷ _____ = _____

b.
54 dots in total

× _____ = _____

÷ _____ = _____

c.
36 dots in total

× _____ = _____

÷ _____ = _____

d.
63 dots in total

× _____ = _____

÷ _____ = _____

**Preparing for Module 9**

Read each problem. Then color the label to show your estimate.

a. Reece ran for 20 minutes and then walked for 37 minutes. About how many minutes did he exercise in total?

| 60 minutes | 70 minutes | 80 minutes |
|---|---|---|

b. Lillian has $72 dollars. She buys some car parts for $51. About how much money does she have left?

| $5 | $10 | $20 |
|---|---|---|

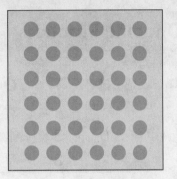

**Step In**    Look at this array.

What is an easy way to calculate the total number of dots?

**42 dots in total**

Look at this picture.

How could you figure out the number of dots in each row?

I could use division. 42 ÷ 6 = ?

But it is easier to think multiplication. 6 × ? = 42

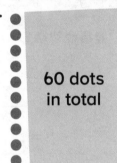

**How could you use multiplication to calculate 30 ÷ 6?**

**Step Up**    1.  Complete the multiplication fact that you would use to figure out the division fact. Then complete the division fact.

**a.**

**12 dots in total**

$2 \times \boxed{\phantom{0}} = 12$

$12 \div 2 = \boxed{\phantom{0}}$

**b.**

**60 dots in total**

$10 \times \boxed{\phantom{0}} = 60$

$60 \div 10 = \boxed{\phantom{0}}$

**c.**

**36 dots in total**

$\boxed{\phantom{0}} \times 6 = 36$

$36 \div 6 = \boxed{\phantom{0}}$

**d.**

**18 dots in total**

$\boxed{\phantom{0}} \times 6 = 18$

$18 \div 6 = \boxed{\phantom{0}}$

**2.** Write facts to match.

**a.**

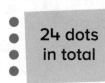

24 dots in total

___ × ___ = ___

___ ÷ ___ = ___

**b.**

54 dots in total

• • • • • •

___ × ___ = ___

___ ÷ ___ = ___

**c.**

30 dots in total

___ × ___ = ___

___ ÷ ___ = ___

**d.**

21 dots in total

___ × ___ = ___

___ ÷ ___ = ___

**e.**

49 dots in total

• • • • • • • •

___ × ___ = ___

___ ÷ ___ = ___

**f.**

9 dots in total

___ × ___ = ___

___ ÷ ___ = ___

**3.** Write a multiplication fact and division to match this problem.
Use a **?** to show the unknown amount.

Tickets cost $8 each. Ruben paid $48 in total.
How many tickets did he buy?

___ × ___ = ___

___ ÷ ___ = ___

**Step Ahead**   Use the facts on pages 288 and 289 to help solve these
problems. Show your thinking on page 318.

A glass of lemonade uses one lemon.

**a.** Six children each squeezed eight lemons to make
some glasses of lemonade. How many glasses of
lemonade could they make?

_____ glasses

**b.** They sold all the lemonade for $72 in total. If they share
this amount equally, how much money will they each get?

$_____

**Step In**

A group of friends has been asked to arrange **60** chairs into equal rows.

You could have 12 chairs in each row, or

3 rows of 20, or

6 equal rows.

How can you figure out if each of these shares is possible?

**Color an array below to show another way to arrange the chairs.**

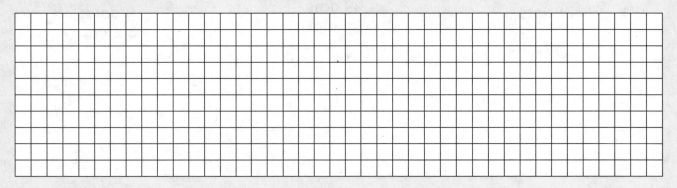

**What fact family could you write to describe the share?**

**Step Up**

1. Color an array to match the numbers given.
Then complete the fact family to match.

a.

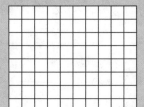

7 × 6 = _____

____ × ____ = ____

____ ÷ ____ = ____

____ ÷ ____ = ____

b.

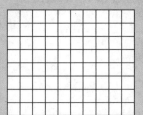

8 × 6 = _____

____ × ____ = ____

____ ÷ ____ = ____

____ ÷ ____ = ____

c.

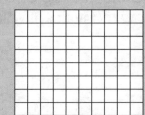

6 × 2 = _____

____ × ____ = ____

____ ÷ ____ = ____

____ ÷ ____ = ____

**2.** Complete each fact. Then draw lines to connect facts from the same family. Cross out the two facts that do not have a match.

18 ÷ 3 = ☐     ☐ = 18 ÷ 6

9 × 6 = ☐     6 × 7 = ☐

☐ = 24 ÷ 4     ☐ = 7 × 8

42 ÷ 7 = ☐     54 ÷ 6 = ☐

☐ = 7 × 7     6 × 4 = ☐

24 ÷ 8 = ☐     49 ÷ 7 = ☐

**3.** Write the missing number in each fact.

**a.**
60 ÷ 6 = ☐

**b.**
☐ ÷ 6 = 6

**c.**
21 ÷ ☐ = 3

**d.**
24 ÷ ☐ = 6

**e.**
☐ ÷ 9 = 6

**f.**
7 = ☐ ÷ 6

**g.**
0 ÷ 6 = ☐

**h.**
1 = ☐ ÷ 3

---

**Step Ahead**     Circle each box of stickers that you think can be equally shared among six. Show your thinking on page 318.

 80 STICKERS

90 STICKERS

 120 STICKERS

 100 STICKERS

© ORIGO Education

**Think and Solve**

The numbers in the circles are the sums of the rows and the columns.

Same letters are the same numbers.
Write the value for each letter.

A = ☐    B = ☐

C = ☐    D = ☐

E = ☐    F = ☐

Start with a row or column that has all the same letters.

| A | B | A | A | 15 |
|---|---|---|---|---|
| D | B | C | B | 24 |
| 8 | 12 | E | F | |

**Words at Work**

Write a word problem that involves a sixes division fact.
Then write how you find the solution.

_____

_____

_____

_____

_____

_____

_____

_____

_____

_____

**Ongoing Practice**    **I.** Complete these standard addition algorithms.

a.

| H | T | O |
|---|---|---|
|   |   |   |
| 2 | 4 | 8 |
| + |   |   |
|   | 2 | 7 |

b.

| H | T | O |
|---|---|---|
|   |   |   |
| 4 | 1 | 6 |
| + |   |   |
|   | 5 | 6 |

c.

| H | T | O |
|---|---|---|
|   |   |   |
|   | 3 | 6 |
| + |   |   |
|   | 8 | 3 |

d.

| H | T | O |
|---|---|---|
|   |   |   |
|   | 4 | 5 |
| + |   |   |
|   | 9 | 2 |

e.

| H | T | O |
|---|---|---|
|   |   |   |
| 3 | 1 | 8 |
| + |   |   |
| 1 | 5 | 7 |

f.

| H | T | O |
|---|---|---|
|   |   |   |
| 4 | 7 | 2 |
| + |   |   |
| 2 | 5 | 6 |

**2.** Write facts to match.

a.

18 dots
in total

_____ × _____ = _____

_____ ÷ _____ = _____

b.

54 dots
in total

_____ × _____ = _____

_____ ÷ _____ = _____

c.

42 dots
in total

_____ × _____ = _____

_____ ÷ _____ = _____

**Preparing for Module 9**    Calculate the difference. Draw jumps on the number line to show your thinking.

a.

65 – 27 = _____

◄─────────────────────────────────────►

b.

72 – 35 = _____

◄─────────────────────────────────────►

**Step In**

Eight friends shared a pizza.
Each friend had one-eighth of the whole pizza.

What fraction can you write to show how many eighths were eaten? ____

What is another way of describing how much pizza was eaten?

$\frac{8}{8}$ is the same value as one whole.
*One whole* is the same value as 1.

**Step Up**

1. Each strip is one whole. Color parts to show each fraction.

a. $\frac{1}{3}$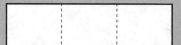

b. $\frac{2}{3}$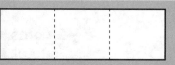

c. $\frac{3}{3}$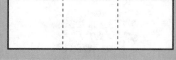

d. $\frac{4}{3}$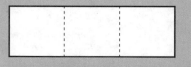

e. $\frac{5}{3}$

f. $\frac{6}{3}$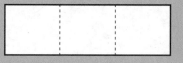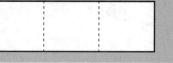

g. $\frac{7}{3}$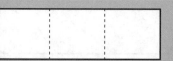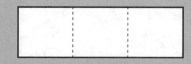

2. Circle the fractions above that represent 1 or 2.

**3.** Each strip is one whole. Color parts to show each fraction.

**a.** one-fourth

**b.** two-fourths

**c.** three-fourths

**d.** four-fourths

**e.** five-fourths

**f.** six-fourths

**g.** seven-fourths

**h.** eight-fourths

**4.** Circle the fractions above that are equal to 1 or 2.

**Step Ahead**   Count by eighths. Write the fractions that you would say.

one-eighth

two-eighths

_____-eighths

_____-eighths

_____-eighths

_____-eighths

_____-eighths

_____-eighths

_____-eighths

# 8.6 Common fractions: Exploring improper fractions

**Step In**

Two strips of paper are placed side by side.
Each strip of paper shows one whole.

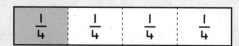

How many fourths have been shaded in total?
How much greater than one whole is that?

An **improper fraction** has a numerator that is equal to or greater than the denominator.
$\frac{5}{5}$ and $\frac{9}{5}$ are both improper fractions.

**Fractions greater than one can also be shown with shapes.**

Each large square on the right is one whole.

Each whole is split into four parts of equal size.

How many fourths are shaded in total?

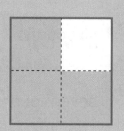

What fraction is shaded?  ———

**Step Up**

1. Each large shape is one whole. Write the fraction that is shaded.

a.

b.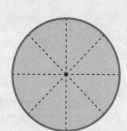

c.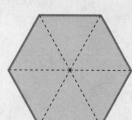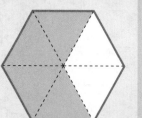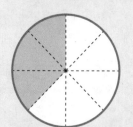

**2.** Each large shape is one whole. Color the shapes to show each fraction.

**a.**

$\frac{6}{4}$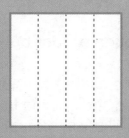

**b.**

$\frac{5}{2}$

**c.**

$\frac{9}{8}$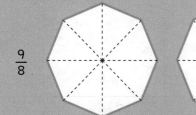

**d.**

$\frac{10}{4}$

**e.**

$\frac{9}{6}$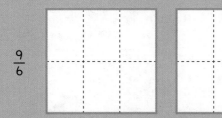

**f.**

$\frac{8}{3}$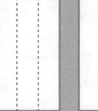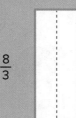

**g.**

$\frac{6}{3}$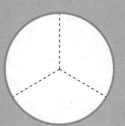

**h.**

$\frac{13}{8}$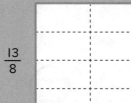

**Step Ahead**

Each square is one whole. Draw lines to split the squares into parts of equal size. Then color parts to show $\frac{9}{4}$.

**ORIGO Stepping Stones** · Grade 3 · 8.6

297 ◆

© ORIGO Education

**Computation Practice**   **What goes through a door but never goes in or out?**

★ Write a multiplication fact you can use to figure out the division fact.
Then write the quotients. Use a ruler to draw a straight line from each quotient on the left to a matching quotient on the right. The line will pass through a number and a letter. Write each letter above its number at the bottom of the page.

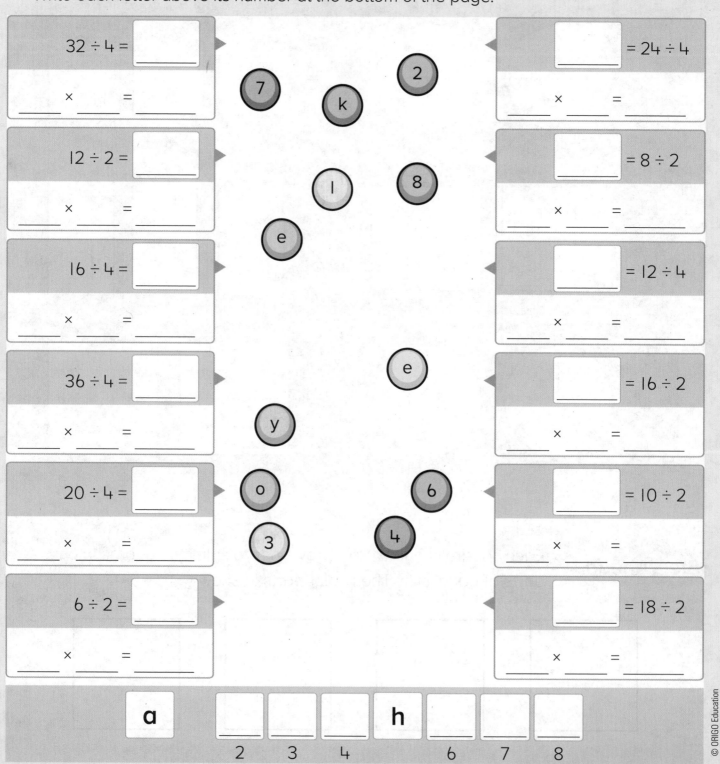

$32 \div 4 = $ ☐

___ × ___ = ___

$12 \div 2 = $ ☐

___ × ___ = ___

$16 \div 4 = $ ☐

___ × ___ = ___

$36 \div 4 = $ ☐

___ × ___ = ___

$20 \div 4 = $ ☐

___ × ___ = ___

$6 \div 2 = $ ☐

___ × ___ = ___

☐ $ = 24 \div 4$

___ × ___ = ___

☐ $ = 8 \div 2$

___ × ___ = ___

☐ $ = 12 \div 4$

___ × ___ = ___

☐ $ = 16 \div 2$

___ × ___ = ___

☐ $ = 10 \div 2$

___ × ___ = ___

☐ $ = 18 \div 2$

___ × ___ = ___

| a |  |  |  | h |  |  |  |
|---|---|---|---|---|---|---|---|
|   | 2 | 3 | 4 |   | 6 | 7 | 8 |

*ORIGO Stepping Stones* · Grade 3 · 8.6

© ORIGO Education

1. Think about how you can change these numbers to make it easier to add. Then complete the equation.

FROM 3.7.11

a.    75 + 98

( is equal to )

_____ + _____ = _____

b.    149 + 46

( is equal to )

_____ + _____ = _____

c.    72 + 128

( is equal to )

_____ + _____ = _____

d.    48 + 137

( is equal to )

_____ + _____ = _____

e.    279 + 31

( is equal to )

_____ + _____ = _____

f.    147 + 39

( is equal to )

_____ + _____ = _____

2. Color an array to match the numbers given. Then complete the fact family to match.

FROM 3.8.4

a.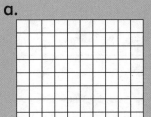

7 × 3 = _____

_____ × _____ = _____

_____ ÷ _____ = _____

_____ ÷ _____ = _____

b.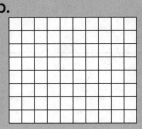

6 × 7 = _____

_____ × _____ = _____

_____ ÷ _____ = _____

_____ ÷ _____ = _____

c.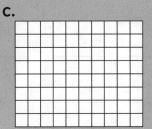

6 × 9 = _____

_____ × _____ = _____

_____ ÷ _____ = _____

_____ ÷ _____ = _____

d.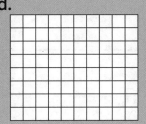

6 × 3 = _____

_____ × _____ = _____

_____ ÷ _____ = _____

_____ ÷ _____ = _____

**Preparing for Module 9**

Calculate the difference. Draw jumps on the number line to show your thinking.

147 − 62 = [____]

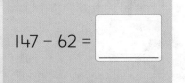

**Step In**

One batch of 12 muffins needs $\frac{2}{3}$ cup of mashed banana.

Maka wants to make 2 batches but he only has a $\frac{1}{3}$ measuring cup.

What can he do to measure the correct amount of banana for 2 batches of muffins?

> Maka can use the $\frac{1}{3}$ measuring cup two times for one batch, so he can use it four times for two batches.

**How could you show your thinking on a number line?**

What fraction could you write to show the total amount of banana?

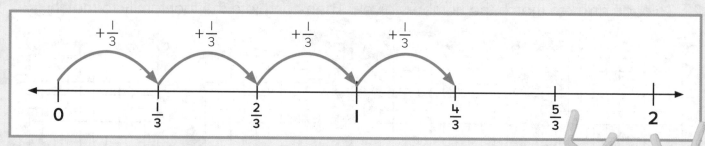

**What do you notice about the fraction $\frac{4}{3}$?**

> The numerator is greater than the denominator.
> I can see on the number line that $\frac{4}{3}$ is greater than 1.

**Step Up**

1. On this number line, the distance from 0 to 1 is one whole. Write the fraction that should be in each box. Draw jumps to help you.

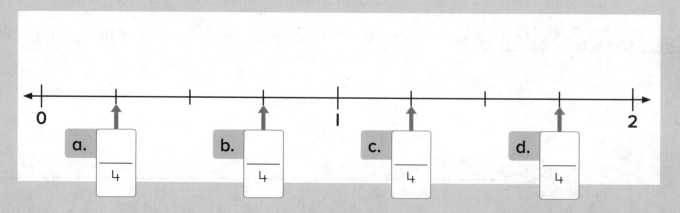

**2.** On each number line, the distance from 0 to 1 is one whole.
Write the fraction that should be in each box. Draw jumps to help you.

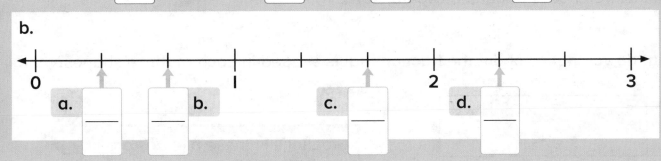

**a.**

**b.**

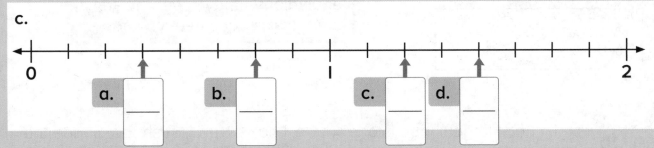

**c.**

**3.** Use the fractions you wrote on the number lines above.

**a.** List the fractions that are less than 1.

**b.** List the fractions that are greater than 1 but less than 2.

---

**Step Ahead**  Complete each equation.

**a.**
$$\frac{1}{4} + \frac{1}{4} + \frac{1}{4} + \frac{1}{4} + \frac{1}{4} = \underline{\quad}$$

**b.**
$$\frac{1}{3} + \frac{1}{3} + \frac{1}{3} + \frac{1}{3} = \underline{\quad}$$

**c.**
$$\frac{1}{6} + \frac{1}{6} + \frac{1}{6} + \frac{1}{6} + \frac{1}{6} + \frac{1}{6} + \frac{1}{6} = \underline{\quad}$$

**d.**
$$\frac{1}{2} + \frac{1}{2} + \frac{1}{2} + \frac{1}{2} + \frac{1}{2} = \underline{\quad}$$

**Step In**

The top shape is one whole. What fraction of it is shaded? How do you know?

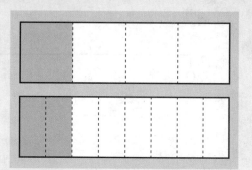

The bottom shape is also one whole.

What fraction of it is shaded?

What do you notice about the two fractions?

**What do you notice about the fraction that is shaded in each of these shapes?**

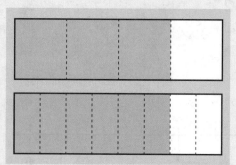

Fractions in these pictures are **equivalent** if they cover the same amount of space in each shape.

**Step Up**

1. Each large shape is one whole. Look at the first shape. Shade the same area on the second shape. Write the fraction of the second shape that is shaded.

a.
$\frac{1}{3}$

is equivalent to

____

b.
$\frac{1}{4}$

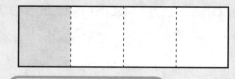

is equivalent to

____

c.
$\frac{1}{2}$

is equivalent to

____

d.
$\frac{1}{2}$

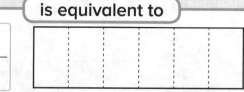

is equivalent to

____

**2.** Each large shape is one whole. Color the first shape to match the fraction. Then color the same area in the second shape and write the equivalent fraction.

**a.**
$\dfrac{2}{4}$

is equivalent to

$\underline{\phantom{xx}}$

**b.**
$\dfrac{2}{3}$

is equivalent to

$\underline{\phantom{xx}}$

**c.**
$\dfrac{6}{8}$

is equivalent to

$\underline{\phantom{xx}}$

**d.**
$\dfrac{2}{2}$

is equivalent to

$\underline{\phantom{xx}}$

**3.** Use the shapes from Questions 1 and 2 to help you write equivalent fractions.

**a.** $\dfrac{\phantom{x}}{2} = \dfrac{2}{4}$

**b.** $\dfrac{\phantom{x}}{8} = \dfrac{1}{4}$

**c.** $\dfrac{\phantom{x}}{3} = \dfrac{6}{6}$

**d.** $\dfrac{2}{2} = \dfrac{\phantom{x}}{8}$

**Step Ahead**

Look at the shape on the left. Write the fraction that is shaded. Then draw more lines on the shape on the right to show an equivalent fraction.

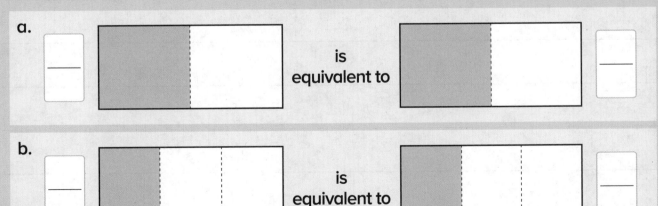

**a.**
$\underline{\phantom{xx}}$

is equivalent to

$\underline{\phantom{xx}}$

**b.**
$\underline{\phantom{xx}}$

is equivalent to

$\underline{\phantom{xx}}$

## Think and Solve

Ruth can move two shapes so that there are 12 kilograms on each scale.

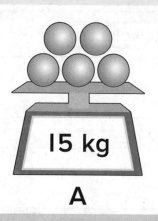  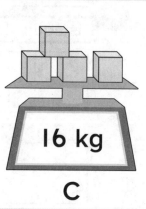

| 15 kg | 5 kg | 16 kg |
|:---:|:---:|:---:|
| **A** | **B** | **C** |

**a.** Which two shapes can she move?

**b.** Where can she move them?

## Words at Work

Write two equivalent fractions.

$$\frac{\ }{\ } \qquad \frac{\ }{\ }$$

Write how you know the two fractions are equivalent.

## Ongoing Practice

1. Solve each problem. Show your thinking.

**a.** A florist sells 258 bunches of flowers in one week and 147 in the next week. How many bunches were sold in total?

_____ bunches

**b.** Jamar sends 353 packages over two weeks. In one week, he sent 164 packages. How many did he send in the other week?

_____ packages

2. Each strip is one whole. Color parts to show each fraction.

**a.** two-halves

**b.** three-halves

**c.** four-halves

**d.** five-halves

## Preparing for Module 9

Think about how you can change these numbers to make it easier to add. Then complete the sentence.

**a.** 48 + 72

is equal to

_____ + _____ = _____

**b.** 18 + 158

is equal to

_____ + _____ = _____

**Step In**

On each number line, the distance from 0 to I is one whole.
What fraction is the arrow pointing to? How do you know?

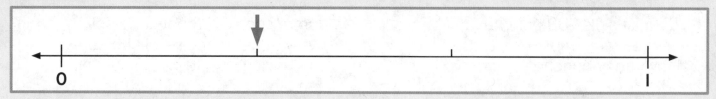

This number line is also split into parts.

What fraction is the arrow below pointing to? How do you know?

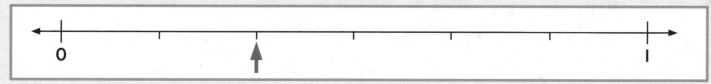

**What can you say about the fractions at each arrow?**

Complete this equation to show how the fractions are equivalent.

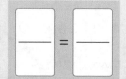

On a number line, fractions are **equivalent** if they are the same distance from zero.

This number line is split into thirds and sixths.
What pair of equivalent fractions does it show?

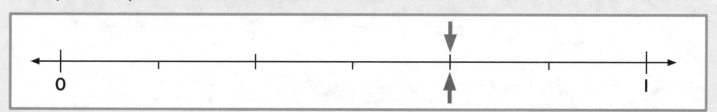

**Step Up**

I. On each number line, the distance from 0 to I is one whole.
Write the fraction shown by the arrow above the line. Then write the equivalent fraction shown below.

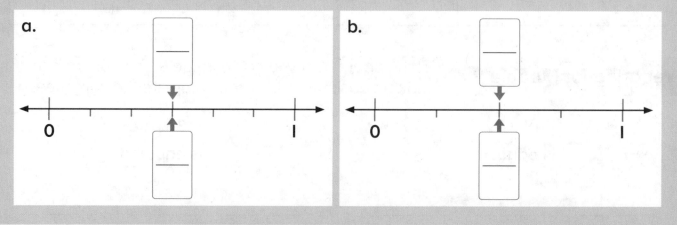

a.

b.

**2.** On each number line, the distance from 0 to 1 is one whole. Draw a line from each fraction to its position on the number line. Then write the equivalent fractions.

**a.** $\dfrac{2}{3} = \dfrac{4}{6}$   **b.** $\dfrac{8}{3} = \underline{\phantom{00}}$   **c.** $\dfrac{10}{6} = \underline{\phantom{00}}$   **d.** $\dfrac{18}{6} = \underline{\phantom{00}}$

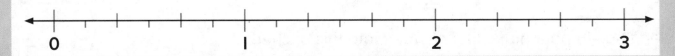

0          1          2          3

**e.** $\dfrac{3}{2} = \underline{\phantom{00}}$   **f.** $\dfrac{4}{2} = \underline{\phantom{00}}$   **g.** $\dfrac{5}{2} = \underline{\phantom{00}}$   **h.** $\dfrac{8}{2} = \underline{\phantom{00}}$

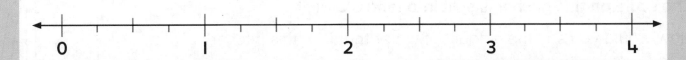

0          1          2          3          4

**3.** Circle all the fractions that are equivalent to 2.

$\dfrac{8}{8}$        $\dfrac{12}{4}$        $\dfrac{12}{6}$        $\dfrac{9}{3}$        $\dfrac{4}{2}$        $\dfrac{14}{8}$

---

**Step Ahead**   On this number line, the distance from 0 to 1 is one whole. Draw a line from each fraction to show where it is located on the number line.

$\dfrac{1}{5}$          $\dfrac{3}{5}$          $\dfrac{5}{5}$          $\dfrac{4}{5}$

0                                                                    1

© ORIGO Education

## Step In

**How much water is in this pitcher? How can you tell?**

I looked at the scale. The water line reaches the end of the scale, so the pitcher must hold one liter.

Selena has to pour **half** a liter of water into this pitcher.

Mark the half-liter position on the scale of the pitcher.
How did you decide where to draw the mark?

How would you show **one-fourth** of a liter on the same scale?
How would you show **three-fourths** of a liter?

**The scale on this pitcher is split into tenths of a liter.**

How would you say the amount of water that is in this pitcher?

Mark the position on the scale that shows $\frac{7}{10}$ of a liter.

## Step Up

I.   Write the amount of juice in each pitcher as a fraction of one liter.

a.

____ L

b.

____ L

c.

____ L

**2.** Write the amount of water in each pitcher as a fraction of one liter.

a. 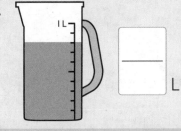 _____ L

b. 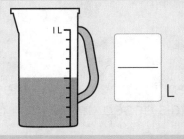 _____ L

c. 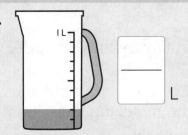 _____ L

**3.** Color the pitcher to match each fraction.

a. 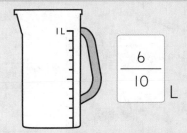 $\dfrac{6}{10}$ L

b. 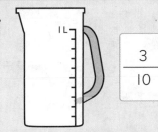 $\dfrac{3}{10}$ L

c. 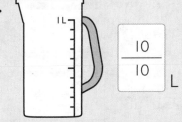 $\dfrac{10}{10}$ L

**4.** Solve this problem. Color the pitcher to help your thinking.

The pitcher holds one liter of water. 2 glasses of water are poured from the pitcher. There is now $\dfrac{4}{10}$ of a liter of water left in the pitcher. How much water was poured from the pitcher?

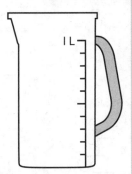

_____ L

---

**Step Ahead**

Circle the fraction that shows the greater amount of water. Color the pitchers to help your thinking.

a.
$\dfrac{3}{4}$ L    **or**    $\dfrac{5}{10}$ L

b.
$\dfrac{4}{10}$ L    **or**    $\dfrac{1}{4}$ L

### Computation Practice

★ Complete the equations. Then find each total in the puzzle below and shade the matching letter. Some totals appear more than once.

146 + 37 = _____

63 + 118 = _____

57 + 117 = _____

237 + 48 = _____

275 + 26 = _____

136 + 57 = _____

323 + 68 = _____

217 + 46 = _____

114 + 76 = _____

18 + 253 = _____

28 + 326 = _____

137 + 18 = _____

134 + 27 = _____

37 + 258 = _____

## Ongoing Practice

**1.** A **pyramid** has many triangular faces that meet at the same point. Circle the pyramids.

a.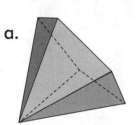

b.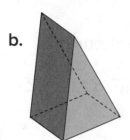

c.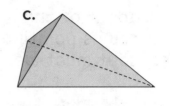

d.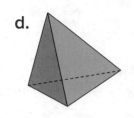

**2.** Each large shape is one whole. Write the fraction that is shaded.

a.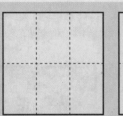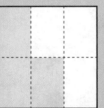

b.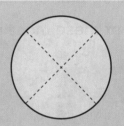

c.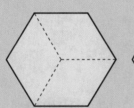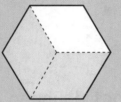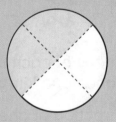

## Preparing for Module 9

The distance from 0 to 1 is one whole.
Look at the number of parts on the number lines.
Write the fraction that should be in each box.

a.    b.    c.    d.    e.    f.

0                          1

g.    h.    i.    j.    k.    l.    m.    n.

0                          1

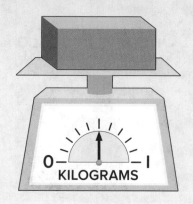

**Step In**

How much does this package weigh?
How can you tell?

The readout of this scale is curved. The arrow is pointing at the halfway point, so it must weigh half a kilogram.

Draw an arrow to show $\frac{8}{10}$ of a kilogram on this scale.

**Grams** are often used to measure amounts that are less than one kilogram. One kilogram is equal to 1,000 grams.

**Look at these mass pieces.**

A short way to write grams is **g**.

How many of each mass piece do you need to balance one kilogram?

What fraction of one kilogram does each mass piece balance?

What doubling and halving pattern can you see?

**Step Up**

1. Write each mass as a fraction of one kilogram.

**a.**

KILOGRAMS

$\frac{}{10}$ kg

**b.**

KILOGRAMS

$\frac{}{}$ kg

**c.**

KILOGRAMS

$\frac{}{}$ kg

**2.** Color the mass pieces you would need to make one kilogram.

**a.**

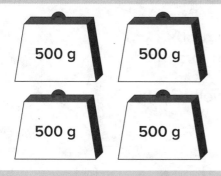

**b.**

**c.**

**d.**

**3.** Write how many  50 g pieces would be needed to balance these mass pieces.

**a.**

500 g

_____

**b.**

250 g

_____

**c.**

200 g

_____

**d.**

100 g

_____

---

**Step Ahead**    Figure out the mass of each cylinder.

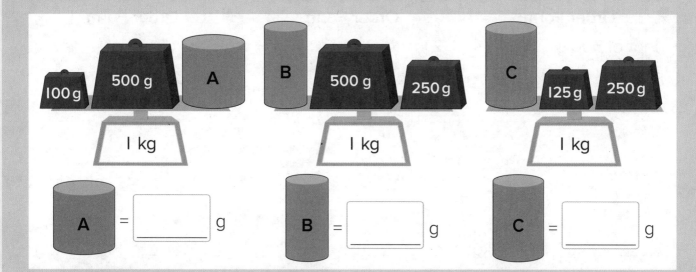

A = _____ g

B = _____ g

C = _____ g

**Step In**

Connor packs small jars of jelly into a box.
He weighs the box when there are 5 jars inside.

How many grams do you think the 5 jars together weigh?

Wetl I know 2 jars will weigh 100 grams.
I can build up from there.

Connor delivers the box of jars to his local grocer.
The grocer takes three jars from the box to place them on the shelf.

How much do the remaining jars together now weigh?

How would you say the mass
as a fraction of one kilogram?

**Step Up**

1. Calculate the total mass of each order.
Write the total in grams, then as a
fraction of one kilogram.

| 🔎 Order Form | 🔎 Order Form | 🔎 Order Form |
|---|---|---|
| 1 jar of 500 g | 2 jars of 250 g | 4 jars of 100 g |
| 3 jars of 100 g | 1 jar of 100 g | 1 jar of 500 g |
| _____ g   [ /10 ] kg | _____ g   [ /10 ] kg | _____ g   [ /10 ] kg |

© ORIGO Education

**2.** Solve each problem. Show your thinking.

**a.** Three jars are packed into one bag. Two of the jars each weigh 200 g. The third jar weighs 500 g. What is the total mass of the three jars?

_____ g

**b.** A pitcher holds one liter of water. The water from the pitcher is poured equally into 8 small glasses. What fraction of a liter is in each glass?

[  ⎯  ] L

**c.** A recipe uses 5 grams of jelly for each muffin. How many muffins can be made with 40 grams of jelly?

_____ muffins

**d.** A box of jars weighs 800 g in total. 2 jars are taken out of the box. Each of these jars weigh 100 g. How much does the box of jars now weigh?

_____ g

**Step Ahead**

Vishaya visits a grocery store in Canada. She buys $\frac{3}{4}$ kg of apples, $\frac{1}{2}$ kg of oranges, and 250 g of grapes. The fruit is packed together in a shopping bag.

What is the total mass of the fruit?

_____ g

## Think and Solve

 Read the directions first.

Use a ruler to draw a line to make two parts the **same** size and shape.

The sum of the numbers in each part must be the same.

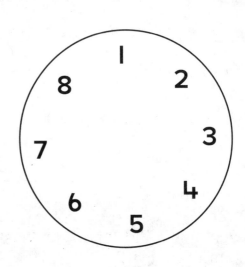

## Words at Work

Choose and write words from the list to complete these sentences. Some words are not used.

> one-half
> denominator
> mass
> equivalent
> capacity
> numerator
> grams
> one-fourth

a. One kilogram is equal to 1,000 _____.

b. A liter is a unit of _____.

c. Fractions are _____ on a number line if they are the same distance from zero.

d. 500 grams is equal to _____ of a kilogram.

e. An improper fraction has a _____ that is equal to or greater than the _____.

## Ongoing Practice

**1.** Complete this chart.

| Object | Vertices | Straight edges | Curved edges | Flat faces | Curved surfaces |
|---|---|---|---|---|---|
| a. 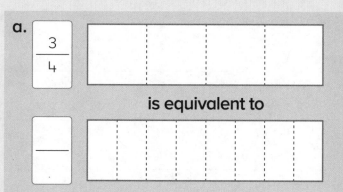 | 4 | | | | 0 |
| b. 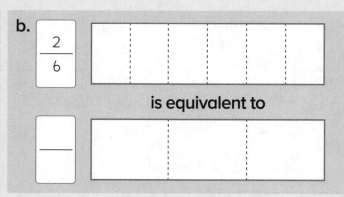 | | | 0 | | |

**2.** Color the shapes and write the fractions to match.

a.

$\dfrac{3}{4}$

is equivalent to

$\dfrac{\quad}{\quad}$

b.

$\dfrac{2}{6}$

is equivalent to

$\dfrac{\quad}{\quad}$

## Preparing for Module 9

On each number line, the distance from 0 to 1 is one whole. Split each number line into more parts to help find equivalent fractions.

a.

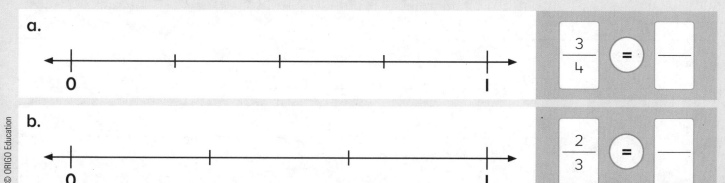

0          1

$\dfrac{3}{4}$ = $\dfrac{\quad}{\quad}$

b.

0                    1

$\dfrac{2}{3}$ = $\dfrac{\quad}{\quad}$

## Step In

It is not always necessary to give an exact answer. Estimates are sometimes just as useful.

Smallfield  45 miles →
Granton  64 miles →
Stryker  92 miles →

About how much farther is Granton than Smallfield?

What is your estimate of the distance from Smallfield to Stryker?

I know double 45 is 90, so it must be a little more than 45 miles.

Sometimes it's easier to use addition than to use subtraction. Think 45 + ___ = 92.

## Step Up

I. Estimate the distance between these towns.

**a.** The distance from Barton to Moonby

is about _____ miles.

The distance from Moonby to Leyburn

is about _____ miles.

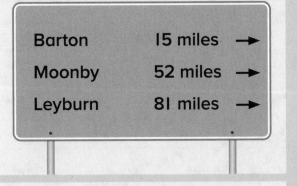

Barton  15 miles →
Moonby  52 miles →
Leyburn  81 miles →

**b.** The distance from Saxville to Belding

is about _____ miles.

The distance from Belding to Chapin

is about _____ miles.

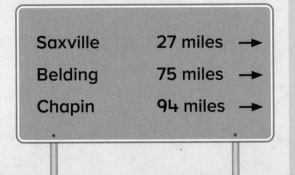

Saxville  27 miles →
Belding  75 miles →
Chapin  94 miles →

**2.** Estimate the distance between these towns.

**a.** The distance from Hibbing to Canton

is about [____] miles.

The distance from Canton to Gann

is about [____] miles.

The distance from Canton to Thayer

is about [____] miles.

| Hibbing | 9 miles | → |
| Canton | 46 miles | → |
| Gann | 51 miles | → |
| Thayer | 83 miles | → |

**b.** The distance from Findley to Gowen

is about [____] miles.

The distance from Gowen to Upston

is about [____] miles.

The distance from Upston to McRae

is about [____] miles.

| Findley | 19 miles | → |
| Gowen | 57 miles | → |
| Upston | 85 miles | → |
| McRae | 99 miles | → |

**Step Ahead**   Look at the directions.
Estimate the distances.

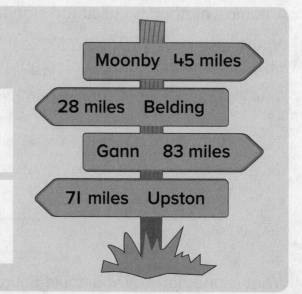

Moonby   45 miles

28 miles   Belding

Gann   83 miles

71 miles   Upston

**a.** The distance between Moonby and Gann

is about [____] miles.

**b.** The distance from Belding to Upston

is about [____] miles.

**Step In**

Jacob and Antonio used different methods to calculate the difference between 578 and 263.

How are their methods the same? How are they different?

### Jacob's method

| Step 1 | | | |
|---|---|---|---|
| H | T | O |
| 5 | 7 | 8 |
| – | | | 3 |
| 5 | 7 | 5 |
| – | | | |
| | | | |
| – | | | |

| Step 2 | | | |
|---|---|---|---|
| H | T | O |
| 5 | 7 | 8 |
| – | | | 3 |
| 5 | 7 | 5 |
| – | | 6 | 0 |
| 5 | 1 | 5 |
| – | | | |

| Step 3 | | | |
|---|---|---|---|
| H | T | O |
| 5 | 7 | 8 |
| – | | | 3 |
| 5 | 7 | 5 |
| – | | 6 | 0 |
| 5 | 1 | 5 |
| – | 2 | 0 | 0 |
| 3 | 1 | 5 |

### Antonio's method

| Step 1 | | |
|---|---|---|
| H | T | O |
| 5 | 7 | 8 |
| – 2 | 6 | 3 |
| | | 5 |

| Step 2 | | |
|---|---|---|
| H | T | O |
| 5 | 7 | 8 |
| – 2 | 6 | 3 |
| | 1 | 5 |

| Step 3 | | |
|---|---|---|
| H | T | O |
| 5 | 7 | 8 |
| – 2 | 6 | 3 |
| 3 | 1 | 5 |

**Antonio's method is called the standard algorithm for subtraction.**

Where else have you heard the word algorithm?
How is the standard addition algorithm the same as the standard subtraction algorithm?

How do you think the subtraction algorithm works with these problems?

| H | T | O |
|---|---|---|
| 3 | 6 | 7 |
| – | 2 | 5 |
| | | |

| H | T | O |
|---|---|---|
| 6 | 4 | 5 |
| – | | 3 |
| | | |

| T | O |
|---|---|
| 8 | 4 |
| – 5 | 3 |
| | |

| T | O |
|---|---|
| 5 | 8 |
| – | 6 |
| | |

What is another way you could figure out some of these problems?

Estimate the difference between the two prices. Then use the standard subtraction algorithm to calculate the exact difference.

**a.**

Estimate $_____

| H | T | O |
|---|---|---|
| 7 | 6 | 9 |
| − 2 | 3 | 8 |
| | | |

**b.**

Estimate $_____

| T | O |
|---|---|
| | |
| − | |
| | |

**c.**

Estimate $_____

| H | T | O |
|---|---|---|
| | | |
| − | | |
| | | |

**d.**

Estimate $_____

| T | O |
|---|---|
| | |
| − | |
| | |

**e.**

Estimate $_____

| H | T | O |
|---|---|---|
| | | |
| − | | |
| | | |

**f.**

Estimate $_____

| H | T | O |
|---|---|---|
| | | |
| − | | |
| | | |

**g.**

Estimate $_____

| H | T | O |
|---|---|---|
| | | |
| − | | |
| | | |

**h.**

Estimate $_____

| H | T | O |
|---|---|---|
| | | |
| − | | |
| | | |

**Step Ahead**

Morgan used the standard algorithm to calculate the difference between these prices.

Write in words the mistake that she made.

| H | T | O |
|---|---|---|
| 4 | 8 | 5 |
| − 3 | 2 | |
| 1 | 6 | 5 |

_____

_____

_____

**Computation Practice**    The longer it goes, the shorter it grows.

★ Complete the equations. Then write each letter above its matching total at the bottom of the page. Some letters appear more than once.

| | | | |
|---|---|---|---|
| 56 + 57 = ____ | **g** | 67 + 68 = ____ | **n** |
| 77 + 75 = ____ | **l** | 85 + 87 = ____ | **r** |
| 96 + 98 = ____ | **i** | 58 + 57 = ____ | **e** |
| 66 + 68 = ____ | **u** | 86 + 88 = ____ | **c** |
| 97 + 95 = ____ | **b** | 75 + 76 = ____ | **a** |
| 67 + 65 = ____ | **d** | | |

**Working Space**

| 151 | 192 | 134 | 172 | 135 | 194 | 135 | 113 |

| 174 | 151 | 135 | 132 | 152 | 115 |

## Ongoing Practice

**I.** Write the amount of water in each container as a fraction of a liter.

**a.**
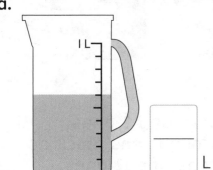
| | L

**b.**
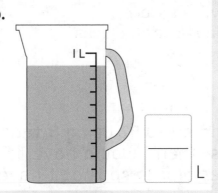
| | L

**c.**

| | L

**2.** Estimate the distance between these towns.

**a.** The distance from Ashford to Oxford

is about [ ] miles.

**b.** The distance from Oxford to Weston

is about [ ] miles.

**c.** The distance between Ashford to Weston

is about [ ] miles.

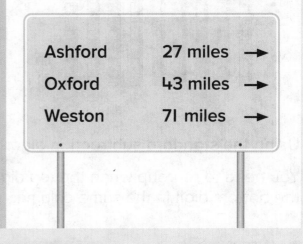

| Ashford | 27 miles | → |
| Oxford | 43 miles | → |
| Weston | 71 miles | → |

## Preparing for Module 10

Use your ruler to draw equal rows and columns of squares. Then write the total number of squares in each rectangle.

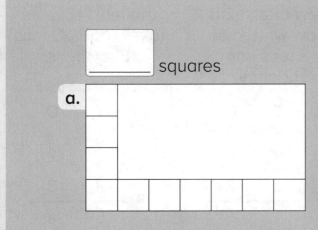

[ ] squares

**a.**

**b.**

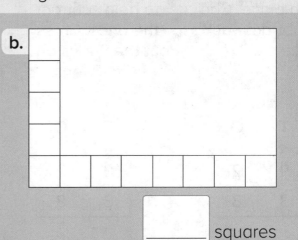

[ ] squares

**Step In**

Dorothy has $92 and buys this game.

How much money will she have left over?
How could you calculate it using base-10 blocks?

I would show 92 using 9 tens blocks and 2 ones blocks. Then I would have to regroup 1 tens block as 10 ones blocks so that I have 8 tens and 12 ones.

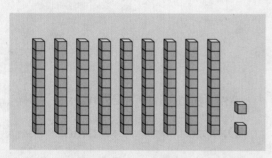  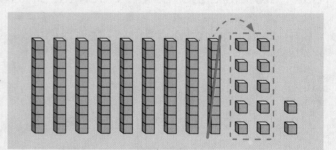

**Using the standard subtraction algorithm is like using base-10 blocks.**

You need to regroup when the top digit in a place-value column is less than the bottom digit in the same column.

| Step 1 | Step 2 | Step 3 | Step 4 |
|---|---|---|---|
| Look at the digits in each place. Can you subtract each place easily? | You need 1 ten to help subtract the ones. Cross out the 9 tens and write 8 tens. | Cross out the ones digit and write the new total. 92 is now written as 8 tens and 12 ones. | Subtract the ones, then subtract the tens. 12 ones take 8 ones. 8 tens take 3 tens. |

| | T | O | | T | O | | T | O | | T | O |
|---|---|---|---|---|---|---|---|---|---|---|---|
| | | | | | 8 | | | 8 | 12 | | 8 | 12 |
| | 9 | 2 | | 9̶ | 2 | | 9̶ | 2̶ | | 9̶ | 2̶ |
| − | 3 | 8 | − | 3 | 8 | − | 3 | 8 | − | 3 | 8 |
| | | | | | | | | | | 5 | 4 |

1. Change the blocks to show the regrouping. Then change the numbers and use the standard subtraction algorithm to calculate the difference.

a.
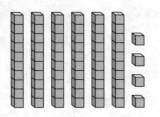

|   | T | O |
|---|---|---|
|   | 6 | 4 |
| − | 3 | 7 |

b.
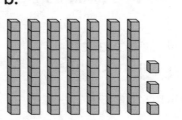

|   | T | O |
|---|---|---|
|   | 7 | 3 |
| − | 4 | 6 |

c.
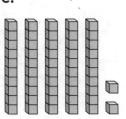

|   | T | O |
|---|---|---|
|   | 5 | 2 |
| − |   | 8 |

d.

|   | T | O |
|---|---|---|
|   | 4 | 5 |
| − | 2 | 9 |

2. Estimate the difference.
Then use the standard subtraction algorithm to calculate the exact difference.

a.
Estimate _____

|   | T | O |
|---|---|---|
|   | 7 | 3 |
| − | 6 | 5 |

b.
Estimate _____

|   | T | O |
|---|---|---|
|   | 4 | 6 |
| − | 1 | 8 |

c.
Estimate _____

|   | T | O |
|---|---|---|
|   | 6 | 2 |
| − | 2 | 7 |

d.
Estimate _____

|   | T | O |
|---|---|---|
|   | 9 | 5 |
| − | 6 | 8 |

Write the missing digits in these standard subtraction algorithms, and regroup when necessary so the answers make sense.

a.

|   | T | O |
|---|---|---|
|   | 5 | 7 |
| − | 2 |   |
|   | 3 | 2 |

b.

|   | T | O |
|---|---|---|
|   |   | 7 |
| − |   | 2 |
|   | 6 | 5 |

c.

|   | T | O |
|---|---|---|
|   | 6 | 4 |
| − |   | 5 |
|   | 1 | 9 |

d.

|   | T | O |
|---|---|---|
|   | 4 |   |
| − |   | 8 |
|   | 3 | 7 |

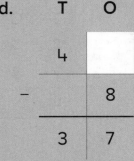

**Step In**

Jayden is at a bookstore and has $283.

MIGHTY MACHINES

Looking After Your Pet

$37

$9

How much money will he have left if he buys the book about machines?

How could you calculate the difference using base-10 blocks?

What would you write using the standard algorithm?

I need more ones so I would regroup I ten as 10 ones. 283 is now written as 2 hundreds, 7 tens, and 13 ones.

| H | T | O |
|---|---|---|
|   | 7 | 13 |
| 2 | 8̶ | 3̶ |
| − |   | 3 | 7 |
| 2 | 4 | 6 |

If Jayden buys the book about pets instead, how much money will he have left?

Use the standard algorithm to show your thinking.

| H | T | O |
|---|---|---|
| − |   |   |
|   |   |   |

I could figure out these problems in my head or use a number line, but using the standard algorithm is good practice for when I need to subtract bigger numbers.

**Step Up**

1. Estimate the difference. Then use the standard subtraction algorithm to calculate the exact difference.

**a.**

Estimate _____

| H | T | O |
|---|---|---|
| 3 | 7 | 3 |
| − |   | 4 | 9 |
|   |   |   |

**b.**

Estimate _____

| H | T | O |
|---|---|---|
| 6 | 5 | 2 |
| − |   | 3 | 7 |
|   |   |   |

**c.**

Estimate _____

| H | T | O |
|---|---|---|
| 5 | 7 | 4 |
| − |   | 4 | 6 |
|   |   |   |

**d.**

Estimate _____

| H | T | O |
|---|---|---|
| 8 | 4 | 6 |
| − |   | 2 | 9 |
|   |   |   |

**2.** Estimate how much money will be left after each purchase.
Then use the standard subtraction algorithm to calculate the exact amount.

**a.**
$35   $472

Estimate $_____

$$-\begin{array}{c}\phantom{0}\\ \hline \phantom{0}\end{array}$$

**b.**
$27   $145

Estimate $_____

$$-\begin{array}{c}\phantom{0}\\ \hline \phantom{0}\end{array}$$

**c.**
$35   $261

Estimate $_____

$$-\begin{array}{c}\phantom{0}\\ \hline \phantom{0}\end{array}$$

**d.**
$18   $352

Estimate $_____

$$-\begin{array}{c}\phantom{0}\\ \hline \phantom{0}\end{array}$$

**e.**
$9   $543

Estimate $_____

$$-\begin{array}{c}\phantom{0}\\ \hline \phantom{0}\end{array}$$

**f.**
$35   $254

Estimate $_____

$$-\begin{array}{c}\phantom{0}\\ \hline \phantom{0}\end{array}$$

**g.**
$27   $175

Estimate $_____

$$-\begin{array}{c}\phantom{0}\\ \hline \phantom{0}\end{array}$$

**h.**
$8   $636

Estimate $_____

$$-\begin{array}{c}\phantom{0}\\ \hline \phantom{0}\end{array}$$

**Step Ahead**   Susan is thinking of a three-digit number.
Jerome is thinking of a two-digit number.

The difference between their numbers is 148.

Write two numbers that
would give that difference.

☐_____  ☐_____

## Think and Solve

Figure out the missing total.

🧸 + 🧸 + 🚗 + 🚗 = $30

🚗 + 🚗 + 🚗 + 🚗 = $20

🧸 + 🧸 + 🚗 = $ _____

## Words at Work

Imagine your friend was away from school when you learned about the standard algorithm for subtraction. Write the steps to calculate 372 − 157 and fill in the algorithm provided.

| H | T | O |
|---|---|---|
| − |   |   |
|   |   |   |

## Ongoing Practice

**I.** Color the container to match the fraction shown.

**a.**
$\dfrac{7}{10}$ L
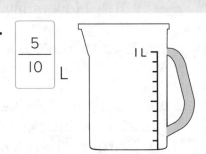

**b.**
$\dfrac{2}{10}$ L
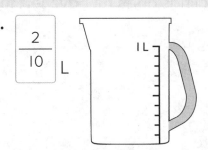

**c.**
$\dfrac{5}{10}$ L
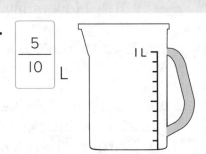

**2.** Use the standard subtraction algorithm to calculate each price difference.

**a.**

$576  $341

| H | T | O |
|---|---|---|
| 5 | 7 | 6 |
| − 3 | 4 | 1 |

**b.**

$42  $87

| T | O |
|---|---|
|  |  |
| − |  |

**c.**
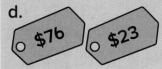
$685  $323

| H | T | O |
|---|---|---|
|  |  |  |
| − |  |  |

**d.**
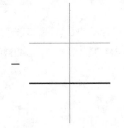
$76  $23

| T | O |
|---|---|
|  |  |
| − |  |

## Preparing for Module 10

Color an array to match the numbers given.
Then complete the fact family.

**a.**

$5 \times 3 = $ ____

____ $\times$ ____ = ____

____ $\div$ ____ = ____

____ $\div$ ____ = ____

**b.**
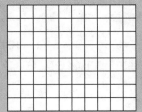

$4 \times 9 = $ ____

____ $\times$ ____ = ____

____ $\div$ ____ = ____

____ $\div$ ____ = ____

**c.**
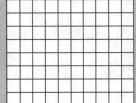

$6 \times 4 = $ ____

____ $\times$ ____ = ____

____ $\div$ ____ = ____

____ $\div$ ____ = ____

**d.**
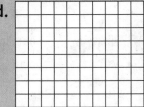

$7 \times 5 = $ ____

____ $\times$ ____ = ____

____ $\div$ ____ = ____

____ $\div$ ____ = ____

## Subtraction: Using the standard algorithm with three-digit numbers (decomposing hundreds)

**Step In**

A gardener had 235 seedlings to plant.
In the first garden bed, he planted 72 seedlings.
How many seedlings does he have left to plant?

How could you calculate it using base-10 blocks?

I would show 235 using
2 hundreds blocks, 3 tens,
and 5 ones. Then I would
take away the number of
seedlings he has planted.

I can take 2 ones from
5 ones but I need to
regroup 1 hundreds
block as 10 tens blocks
so that I have 13 tens.

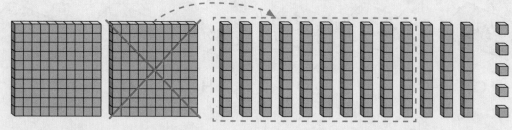

Look at the steps used in this standard subtraction algorithm.
What is happening in each step?

| Step 1 | Step 2 | Step 3 | Step 4 |
|---|---|---|---|
| H T O | H T O | H T O | H T O |
|        | 1      | 1  13  | 1  13  |
| 2 3 5  | 2̷ 3 5 | 2̷ 3̷ 5 | 2̷ 3̷ 5 |
| −   7 2 | −   7 2 | −   7 2 | −   7 2 |
|        |        |        | 1 6 3  |

**Step Up**

1. Estimate the difference. Then use the standard subtraction algorithm to calculate the exact difference.

**a.**

Estimate _____

| H | T | O |
|---|---|---|
| 3 | 2 | 9 |
| − | 5 | 4 |
|   |   |   |

**b.**

Estimate _____

| H | T | O |
|---|---|---|
| 4 | 1 | 5 |
| − | 3 | 2 |
|   |   |   |

**c.**

Estimate _____

| H | T | O |
|---|---|---|
| 6 | 4 | 8 |
| − | 7 | 7 |
|   |   |   |

**d.**

Estimate _____

| H | T | O |
|---|---|---|
| 5 | 3 | 7 |
| − | 8 | 6 |
|   |   |   |

**2.** A zoo has these different snakes on display.

| Snake | Length (cm) |
|---|---|
| Fox Snake | 65 |
| King Cobra | 559 |
| Bushmaster | 261 |
| Coachwhip | 96 |

| Snake | Length (cm) |
|---|---|
| Anaconda | 589 |
| Eastern Indigo | 236 |
| Lyre Snake | 74 |
| Copperhead | 81 |

Use the standard subtraction algorithm to calculate the exact difference in length. Remember to estimate, to check that your answer makes sense.

**a.**

King Cobra
and
Coachwhip

**b.**

Eastern Indigo
and
Copperhead

**c.**

Anaconda
and
Fox Snake

**d.**

Bushmaster
and
Lyre Snake

**e.**

King Cobra
and
Copperhead

**f.**

Anaconda
and
Coachwhip

**Step Ahead**

Snake A is 36 cm longer than Snake B. Snake C is 245 cm long. Snake B is 128 cm shorter than Snake C. How long is each snake?

Snake A is _____ cm   Snake B is _____ cm   Snake C is _____ cm

**Step In**

How would you calculate the difference between each price and the amount in the wallet?

$580

```
    H   T   O
        7   10
    5   8̷   0̷
 -  1   2   6
 _____
```

I can't take 6 ones from 0 ones so I need to regroup 1 ten as 10 ones.

$306

```
    H   T   O
    2   10
    3̷   0̷   6
 -  1   8   2
 _____
```

I can't take 8 tens from 0 tens so I need to regroup 1 hundred as 10 tens.

$475

```
    H   T   O
    4   7   5
 -  1   6   0
 _____
```

I can easily take 0 ones from 5 ones. I don't need to change any digits at all.

**Step Up**

1. Use the standard subtraction algorithm to calculate the exact difference between each pair of prices.

a.

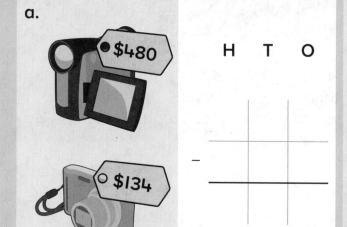

$480

$134

```
    H   T   O


 _____
 -
 _____
```

b.

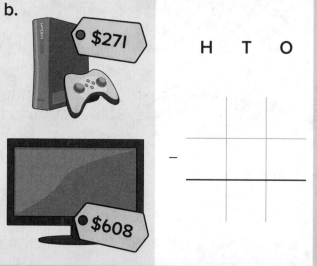

$271

$608

```
    H   T   O


 _____
 -
 _____
```

**2.** Use the standard subtraction algorithm to calculate how much the price has dropped. Remember to estimate, to check that your answer makes sense.

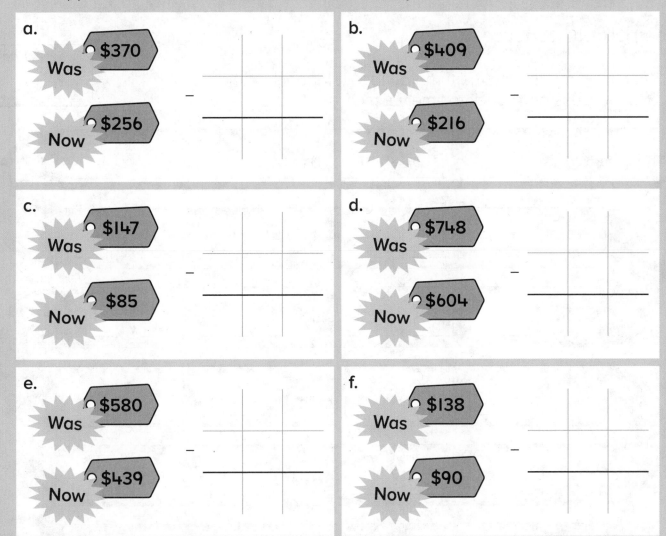

a.
Was $370
Now $256

b.
Was $409
Now $216

c.
Was $147
Now $85

d.
Was $748
Now $604

e.
Was $580
Now $439

f.
Was $138
Now $90

## Step Ahead

Each brick shows the total of the two bricks directly below. Write the missing numbers. You can use page 356 to show your thinking.

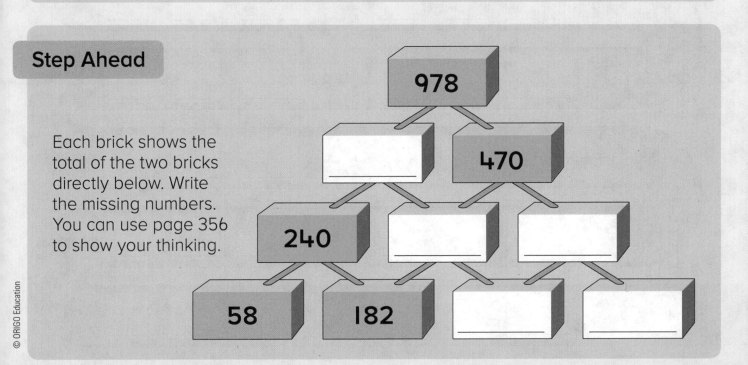

978

470

240

58   182

© ORIGO Education

### Computation Practice

★ Write the product and the turnaround fact for each of these.
Use the classroom clock to time yourself.

Time Taken:

**start**  $6 \times 4 = 24 = 4 \times 6$    $0 \times 7 = \boxed{} = \boxed{} \times \boxed{}$

$1 \times 0 = \boxed{} = \boxed{} \times \boxed{}$    $9 \times 5 = \boxed{} = \boxed{} \times \boxed{}$

$8 \times 9 = \boxed{} = \boxed{} \times \boxed{}$    $4 \times 7 = \boxed{} = \boxed{} \times \boxed{}$

$6 \times 1 = \boxed{} = \boxed{} \times \boxed{}$    $0 \times 3 = \boxed{} = \boxed{} \times \boxed{}$

$5 \times 8 = \boxed{} = \boxed{} \times \boxed{}$    $9 \times 4 = \boxed{} = \boxed{} \times \boxed{}$

$3 \times 8 = \boxed{} = \boxed{} \times \boxed{}$    $2 \times 5 = \boxed{} = \boxed{} \times \boxed{}$

$4 \times 5 = \boxed{} = \boxed{} \times \boxed{}$    $2 \times 8 = \boxed{} = \boxed{} \times \boxed{}$

$5 \times 5 = \boxed{} = \boxed{} \times \boxed{}$    $6 \times 8 = \boxed{} = \boxed{} \times \boxed{}$

$9 \times 2 = \boxed{} = \boxed{} \times \boxed{}$    $1 \times 7 = \boxed{} = \boxed{} \times \boxed{}$

**finish**  $7 \times 5 = \boxed{} = \boxed{} \times \boxed{}$    $9 \times 0 = \boxed{} = \boxed{} \times \boxed{}$

**I.** Color the mass pieces you would need to make one kilogram.

**a.**

| 250 g | 250 g | 250 g | 250 g |
|---|---|---|---|
| 250 g | 250 g | 250 g | 250 g |

**b.**

| 200 g | 200 g | 200 g |
|---|---|---|
| 200 g | 200 g | 200 g |

FROM 3.8.11

**2.** For each of these, use the standard subtraction algorithm to calculate the difference between the price and the amount in the wallet.

**a.** $47    $184

H  T  O

–

**b.** $28    $263

H  T  O

–

**c.** $26    $172

H  T  O

–

**d.** $38    $385

H  T  O

–

FROM 3.9.4

Use a ruler to draw lines to split each shape into **three** rectangles.

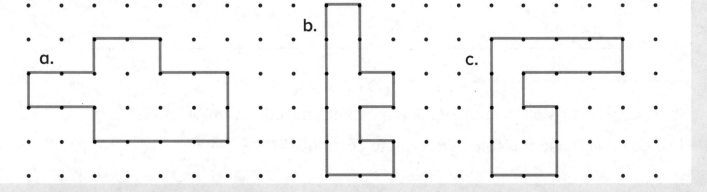

a.

b.

c.

**Step In**  How would you calculate the difference in price between these two cell phones?

$305

$198

I could use the standard algorithm, but there is a lot of regrouping.

Robert shows each number with base-10 blocks.
He then adds the same number of blocks to each group to make it easier to figure out the difference.

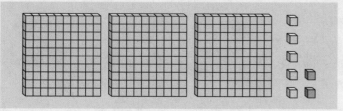
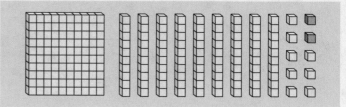

How many ones blocks are added to each group?

What number is now shown by each group of blocks?

How does this make it easier to subtract? Does the difference remain the same?

What happens if the same number of blocks is subtracted from each group?
Does the difference still remain the same?

**Robert shows the same strategy on the number line.**

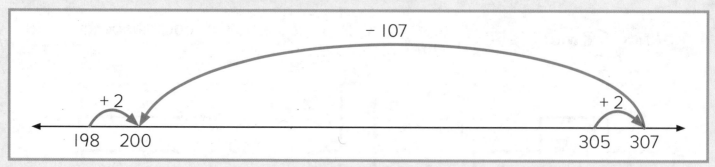

How do the jumps on the number line match his strategy with blocks?

**How could you use the same strategy to calculate 407 − 299?**

**I.** Think about how you can change these numbers to make it easier to subtract. Then complete the sentence.

**a.** 64 − 39   is equal to

___ − ___

**b.** 87 − 52   is equal to

___ − ___

**c.** 129 − 74   is equal to

___ − ___

**d.** 143 − 58   is equal to

___ − ___

**e.** 501 − 398   is equal to

___ − ___

**f.** 305 − 199   is equal to

___ − ___

**2.** Write the difference. Then draw jumps on the number line to show your thinking.

**a.**

82 − 59 = ☐

**b.**

147 − 88 = ☐

**c.**

702 − 498 = ☐

Use the same strategy to solve this problem.

Rita is given $5 to spend at the store. She sees a pencil case that costs $2 and 98 cents and a ruler that costs $1 and 99 cents. She decides to buy the pencil case. How much money does she have left?

$____ and ____¢

**Step In**

Each strip is one whole. What fraction of each strip has been shaded?

Which strip shows the greatest fraction shaded?

Which strip shows the least fraction shaded?

**When you write $\frac{1}{3}$, what does the 3 tell you?**

When you write $\frac{1}{5}$, what does the 5 tell you?

Why is $\frac{1}{5}$ less than $\frac{1}{3}$?

Which fraction is greater in each pair?
How do you know?

| $\frac{1}{8}$ or $\frac{1}{12}$ | | $\frac{1}{20}$ or $\frac{1}{50}$ |

| $\frac{1}{2}$ |
| $\frac{1}{3}$ |
| $\frac{1}{4}$ |
| $\frac{1}{5}$ |
| $\frac{1}{6}$ |
| $\frac{1}{7}$ |
| $\frac{1}{8}$ |

It takes 8 one-eighths to fill one whole and 12 one-twelfths to fill one whole. So eighths are bigger than twelfths.

**Step Up**

I. a. Color one part in each row of this fraction chart.

| 1 | | | | | | | |
| $\frac{1}{2}$ | | | | $\frac{1}{2}$ | | | |
| $\frac{1}{4}$ | | $\frac{1}{4}$ | | $\frac{1}{4}$ | | $\frac{1}{4}$ | |
| $\frac{1}{8}$ | $\frac{1}{8}$ | $\frac{1}{8}$ | $\frac{1}{8}$ | $\frac{1}{8}$ | $\frac{1}{8}$ | $\frac{1}{8}$ | $\frac{1}{8}$ |

b. Circle the fraction that is greater in each pair.

| $\frac{1}{2}$ or $\frac{1}{4}$ | $\frac{1}{8}$ or $\frac{1}{2}$ | $\frac{1}{4}$ or $\frac{1}{8}$ |

**2. a.** Color one part in each row of this fraction chart.

| | | | | | | | | |
|---|---|---|---|---|---|---|---|---|
| $1$ | | | | | | | | |
| $\frac{1}{3}$ | | | $\frac{1}{3}$ | | | $\frac{1}{3}$ | | |
| $\frac{1}{6}$ | | $\frac{1}{6}$ | $\frac{1}{6}$ | | $\frac{1}{6}$ | $\frac{1}{6}$ | | $\frac{1}{6}$ |
| $\frac{1}{9}$ | $\frac{1}{9}$ | $\frac{1}{9}$ | $\frac{1}{9}$ | $\frac{1}{9}$ | $\frac{1}{9}$ | $\frac{1}{9}$ | $\frac{1}{9}$ | $\frac{1}{9}$ |

**b.** Circle the fraction that is greater in each pair.

| $\frac{1}{3}$ **or** $\frac{1}{9}$ | $\frac{1}{6}$ **or** $\frac{1}{3}$ | $\frac{1}{6}$ **or** $\frac{1}{9}$ |
|---|---|---|

**3.** Look at the fractions you circled in Questions 1 and 2. What do you notice?

**4.** Write other fractions to make these sentences true.

**a.** $\frac{1}{2}$ is equivalent to ⬚ which is equivalent to ⬚ .

**b.** $\frac{1}{3}$ is equivalent to ⬚ which is equivalent to ⬚ .

**Step Ahead**

Write these fractions in each sentence to make it true.

$\frac{2}{6}$   $\frac{1}{2}$   $\frac{1}{9}$   $\frac{1}{3}$

**a.** ⬚ is equal to ⬚ which is less than ⬚ which is greater than ⬚ .

**b.** ⬚ is greater than ⬚ which is equal to ⬚ which is greater than ⬚ .

**Think and Solve**  This bag is full of marbles.

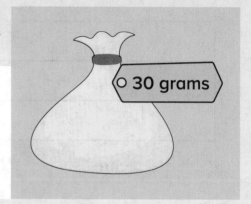

Some of the marbles weigh 2 grams.

Some of the marbles weigh 3 grams.

Some of the marbles weigh 7 grams.

How many of each may be in the bag?

**Words at Work**  Write about two different strategies you could use to solve this equation.

605 – 298 = ?

**Ongoing Practice**

1. Calculate the total mass of each order. Write the total in grams, then as a fraction of one kilogram.

200g   400g   150g

**a.** Order Form

1 jar of 400g

2 jars of 150 g

_____ g   ___ / 10 kg

**b.** Order Form

2 jars of 400g

1 jar of 200 g

_____ g   ___ / 10 kg

**c.** Order Form

4 jars of 150g

1 jar of 200 g

_____ g   ___ / 10 kg

2. Estimate the difference. Then use the standard subtraction algorithm to calculate the exact difference.

**a.**

Estimate _____

| H | T | O |
|---|---|---|
| 3 | 1 | 9 |
| − | 6 | 5 |
|   |   |   |

**b.**

Estimate _____

| H | T | O |
|---|---|---|
| 1 | 3 | 7 |
| − | 5 | 4 |
|   |   |   |

**c.**

Estimate _____

| H | T | O |
|---|---|---|
| 2 | 4 | 6 |
| − | 7 | 3 |
|   |   |   |

**d.**

Estimate _____

| H | T | O |
|---|---|---|
| 1 | 2 | 8 |
| − | 4 | 1 |
|   |   |   |

**Preparing for Module 10**

Write an equation to show each problem. Use a **?** for the unknown amount.

**a.** Amber put up 4 strings of garden lights. Each string had 9 lights. How many lights were there in total?

_____

**b.** Matthew placed 8 packs of water on the store shelf. Each pack had 6 bottles. How many bottles did he place on the shelf?

_____

**Step In**    Three students are talking about fractions on a number line.

Patricia wants to split the line into eighths. Ben wants to split it into sixths, and Paige wants to split it into fourths.

Patricia said that using eighths would mean $\frac{1}{8}$ is the greatest fraction because 8 is greater than 6 and 4. Paige said that the greatest fraction would be $\frac{1}{4}$. Who is correct? How do you know?

**Write < or > to complete each of these.**

$\frac{1}{6} \bigcirc \frac{1}{4}$    $\frac{1}{4} \bigcirc \frac{1}{8}$    $\frac{1}{8} \bigcirc \frac{1}{6}$

**Step Up**    1.  On each number line, the distance from 0 to 1 is one whole.

a.  Write the correct fraction **above** each mark on the number line.

b.  Split the distance from 0 to 1 into eighths and write the correct fraction **below** each mark.

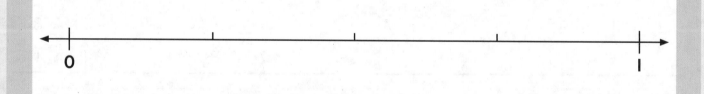

c.  Write the correct fraction **above** each mark on the number line.

d.  Split the distance from 0 to 1 into sixths and write the correct fraction **below** each mark.

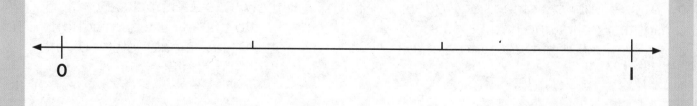

**2.** On each number line, the distance from 0 to 1 is one whole.
Label each blue mark above the number line and each red mark below.
Then write numerals and **<** or **>** to complete the number sentences.

**a.**

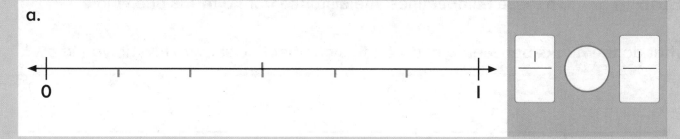

**b.**

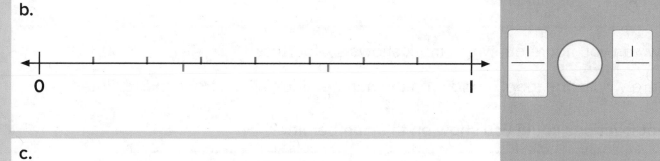

**c.**

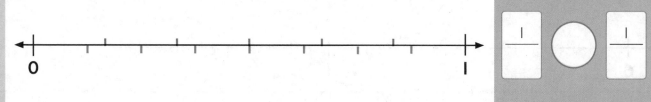

**d.**

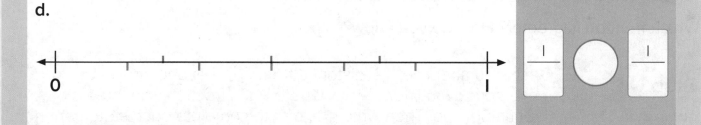

**Step Ahead**

**a.** Split the distance from 0 to 1 into sixteenths and write the correct fraction below each mark.

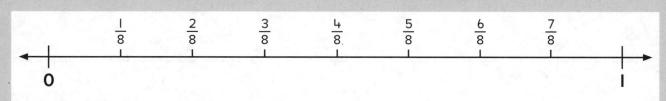

**b.** Complete these equations.

$$\frac{2}{8} = \frac{\phantom{0}}{16} \qquad \frac{\phantom{0}}{16} = \frac{6}{8} \qquad 1 = \frac{\phantom{0}}{16}$$

**Step In**    On these number lines, the distance from 0 to 1 is one whole.

**What do the marks between 0 and 1 on this number line show? How do you know?**

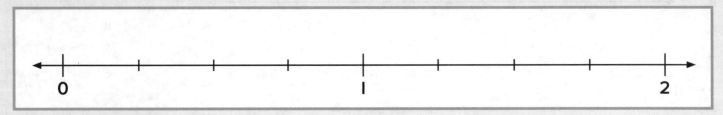

How can you figure out which mark shows six-fourths?

Where would you label $\frac{5}{4}$ and $\frac{7}{4}$ on the number line? Which fraction is greater?

**What fractions could you show on this number line?**

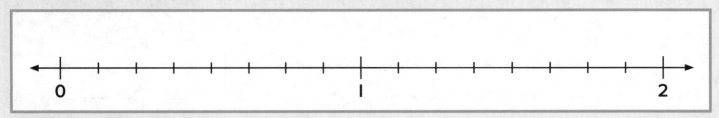

Where would you label $\frac{7}{8}$ and $\frac{10}{8}$ on the number line?

Which fraction is greater? How do you know?

**Step Up**    1. On this number line, the distance from 0 to 1 is one whole. Use a ruler to draw a line to show where each fraction is located on the number line. Then write **<**, **>**, or **=** to complete each statement.

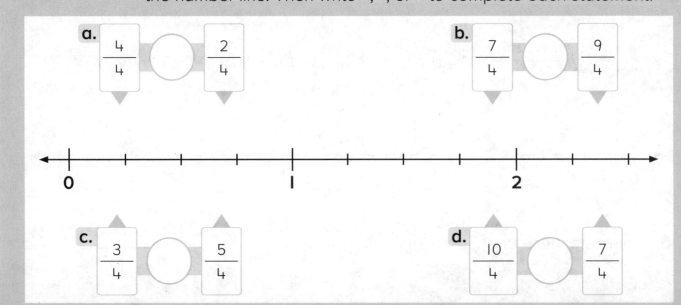

© ORIGO Education

**2.** On each number line, the distance from 0 to 1 is one whole.
For each pair of fractions write **<**, **>**, or **=** to make a true statement.
Use the number lines to help you.

**a.** $\frac{3}{8}$ ◯ $\frac{7}{8}$　**b.** $\frac{6}{8}$ ◯ $\frac{9}{8}$　**c.** $\frac{15}{8}$ ◯ $\frac{12}{8}$　**d.** $\frac{17}{8}$ ◯ $\frac{11}{8}$

0　　　　　　　　　1　　　　　　　　　2

**e.** $\frac{2}{6}$ ◯ $\frac{1}{6}$　**f.** $\frac{7}{6}$ ◯ $\frac{5}{6}$　**g.** $\frac{10}{6}$ ◯ $\frac{12}{6}$　**h.** $\frac{15}{6}$ ◯ $\frac{13}{6}$

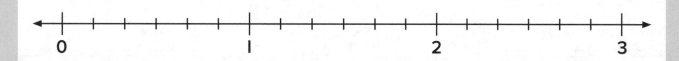

0　　　　　　1　　　　　　2　　　　　　3

**3.** Write **<**, **>**, or **=** to make a true statement.

**a.** $\frac{20}{6}$ ◯ $\frac{18}{6}$　　**b.** $\frac{16}{2}$ ◯ $\frac{9}{2}$　　**c.** $\frac{10}{4}$ ◯ $\frac{12}{4}$

**Step Ahead**

On this number line, the distance from 0 to 1 is one whole. Write a fraction to match each description. Then draw a line from each fraction to show its location on the number line.

**a.** greater than $\frac{4}{4}$
less than $\frac{7}{4}$

**b.** greater than $\frac{10}{4}$
less than $\frac{13}{4}$

**c.** greater than $\frac{15}{4}$
less than $\frac{17}{4}$

**d.** greater than $\frac{17}{4}$
less than $\frac{20}{4}$

0　　　1　　　2　　　3　　　4　　　5

**Computation Practice**    What is the hardest bone in the human body?

★ Write a multiplication fact you can use to figure out each division fact. Then write the quotients. Use a ruler to draw a straight line from each quotient on the left to a matching quotient on the right. The line will pass through a letter and a number. Write each letter above its matching number at the bottom of the page.

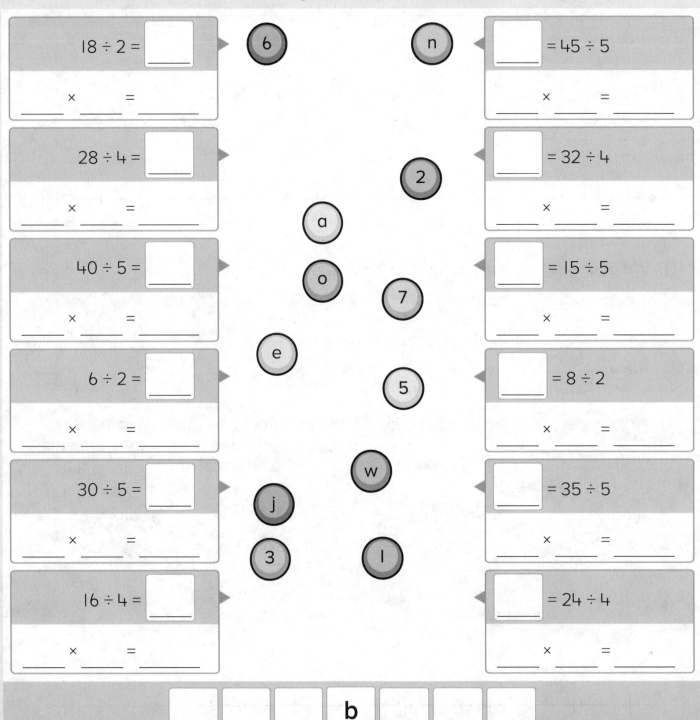

$18 \div 2 =$ ☐

___ × ___ = ___

$28 \div 4 =$ ☐

___ × ___ = ___

$40 \div 5 =$ ☐

___ × ___ = ___

$6 \div 2 =$ ☐

___ × ___ = ___

$30 \div 5 =$ ☐

___ × ___ = ___

$16 \div 4 =$ ☐

___ × ___ = ___

☐ $= 45 \div 5$

___ × ___ = ___

☐ $= 32 \div 4$

___ × ___ = ___

☐ $= 15 \div 5$

___ × ___ = ___

☐ $= 8 \div 2$

___ × ___ = ___

☐ $= 35 \div 5$

___ × ___ = ___

☐ $= 24 \div 4$

___ × ___ = ___

6   n   2   a   o   7   e   5   w   j   3   l

Bottom: ☐ ☐ ☐ **b** ☐ ☐ ☐

1   2   3    5   6   7

## Ongoing Practice

1. Complete these to show matching times.

a.

_____ minutes past _____

_____ minutes to _____

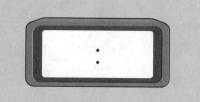

b.

_____ minutes past _____

_____ minutes to _____

5:47

2. On each number line, the distance from 0 to 1 is one whole. Label each mark above the line and each mark below the line. Then write numerals and **<** or **>** to complete true number sentences.

a.

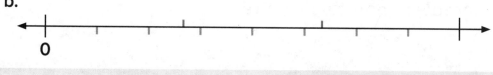

0

$\dfrac{1}{\phantom{0}}$ ◯ $\dfrac{1}{\phantom{0}}$

b.

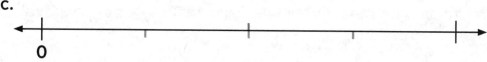

0

$\dfrac{1}{\phantom{0}}$ ◯ $\dfrac{1}{\phantom{0}}$

c.

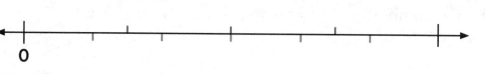

0

$\dfrac{1}{\phantom{0}}$ ◯ $\dfrac{1}{\phantom{0}}$

## Preparing for Module 10

Complete these sentences.

a.

Double ____ is 10

**SO**

Double ____ is 100

b.

Half of 4 is ____

**SO**

Half of 40 is ____

c.

Half of 8 is ____

**SO**

Half of 80 is ____

© ORIGO Education

**Step In**  Order these fractions from greatest to least.

$\frac{1}{8}$  $\frac{1}{4}$  $\frac{1}{6}$  $\frac{1}{2}$  $\frac{1}{3}$

How did you decide the order?

I looked at the denominator. The greater the denominator the smaller the size of the unit fraction.

These fractions have the same numerator. Circle the fraction that is greater.

| $\frac{5}{6}$ or $\frac{5}{8}$ | $\frac{2}{3}$ or $\frac{2}{4}$ | $\frac{3}{4}$ or $\frac{3}{6}$ | $\frac{4}{6}$ or $\frac{4}{8}$ |

How can unit fractions help to compare fractions with the same numerator?

$\frac{1}{3}$ is greater than $\frac{1}{6}$, so two counts of $\frac{1}{3}$ is greater than two counts of $\frac{1}{6}$.

**Step Up**

1. On each number line, the distance from 0 to 1 is one whole. Find each fraction on the number line. Then write **<**, **>**, or **=** to make each statement true.

a.

$\frac{2}{6}$ ◯ $\frac{2}{3}$

0 ⊢———┼———┼———┼———┼———┤ 1

b.
$\frac{3}{4}$ ◯ $\frac{3}{8}$

0 ⊢——┼——┼——┼——┼——┼——┼——┤ 1

**2.** On each number line, the distance from 0 to 1 is one whole. Write **<**, **>**, or **=** to make each statement true. Use the number line to help you.

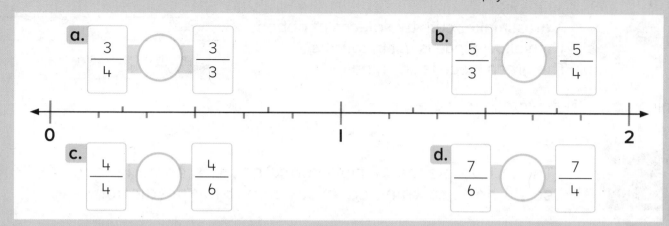

**a.** $\frac{3}{4}$ ◯ $\frac{3}{3}$

**b.** $\frac{5}{3}$ ◯ $\frac{5}{4}$

**c.** $\frac{4}{4}$ ◯ $\frac{4}{6}$

**d.** $\frac{7}{6}$ ◯ $\frac{7}{4}$

**3.** Write **<**, **>**, or **=** to make each statement true. Draw a number line to prove that your answer is correct.

**a.** $\frac{2}{8}$ ◯ $\frac{2}{4}$

**b.** $\frac{5}{2}$ ◯ $\frac{5}{3}$

**c.** $\frac{3}{4}$ ◯ $\frac{3}{2}$

© ORIGO Education

**Step Ahead**   Write denominators to make each statement true.

**a.**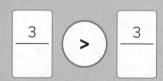

**b.**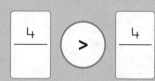

**c.**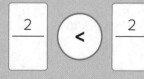

**Step In**

A dressmaker cuts two pieces of ribbon.
The yellow piece is cut in fourths.
The green piece is cut in half.

Which ribbon is cut into longer pieces?

 These two pieces of ribbon are not the same length, so I'll have to think carefully about my prediction.

**Draw a picture to help solve this problem.**

A pine board and a spruce board are the same length. Each board is cut into smaller pieces. The pine is cut into thirds and the spruce is cut into fourths. The pieces are then stacked into one pile. If you laid two of the pine pieces end to end and two of the spruce pieces end to end, which would be longer?

What information helped solve the problem?

What information did not?

**Step Up**

**I.** Solve this problem. Draw a picture to help your thinking.

There are two sticks of celery. Each celery stick is the same length. Amy cuts her celery stick into fourths. Dakota cuts his celery stick into sixths. Both then each eat three pieces of celery. Who ate more celery?

**2.** Solve each problem. Show your thinking.

**a.** Joel and Arleen are running on the same track. Joel runs $\frac{3}{4}$ of the total distance. Arleen runs $\frac{3}{5}$ of the total distance. Who ran the longer distance?

**b.** Two friends are reading the same book. The book has 176 pages. Steven is halfway through the book. Sharon has one-fourth of the book left to read. Who read more pages?

**c.** Yasmin has a ribbon that is half the length of Norton's ribbon. They cut each ribbon into eighths. Norton pastes 3 pieces of ribbon end-to-end on a piece of paper. Yasmin pastes 7 pieces end-to-end on another piece of paper. Who pasted the longer length of ribbon?

**Step Ahead**

Two friends each buy a tub of popcorn at the movies. During the movie, Emilio eats half of his popcorn. Sandra eats about one-fourth of hers. Afterward, they compare the leftover amount of popcorn. They both agree that Emilio has more popcorn left over.

Do you think that this is possible? Explain your thinking in words.

**Think and Solve**  In this diagram, the ⟶ means **is double**.

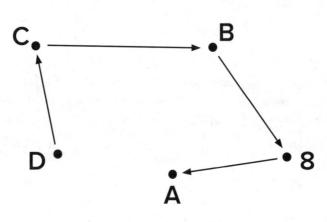

Write the numbers that should be at points A, B, C, and D.

A = _____    B = _____    C = _____    D = _____

**Words at Work**    Write in words how you solve this problem.

Beth and Hiro work together and each week they both earn the same amount. Each week, Beth donates $\frac{1}{5}$ of her earnings to charity, and Hiro donates $\frac{1}{6}$ of his earnings to charity. Who donates more to charity each week?

**Ongoing Practice**

**1.** These clocks show afternoon times on the same day. Calculate the length of each trip.

FROM 3.2.9

**a.**

Bus Departs    Bus Arrives

The trip is [____] minutes long.

**b.**

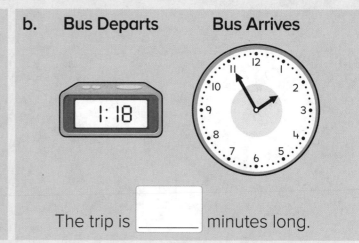

Bus Departs    Bus Arrives

The trip is [____] minutes long.

**2.** On this number line, the distance from 0 to 1 is one whole. For each pair of fractions, write **<**, **>**, or **=** to make a true statement.

FROM 3.9.10

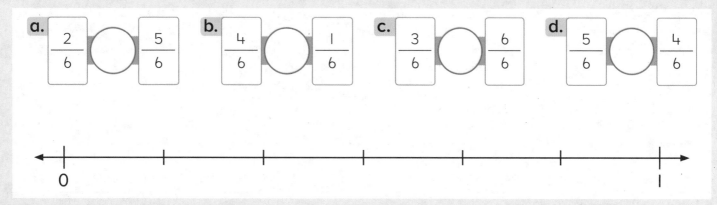

**a.** $\frac{2}{6}$ ◯ $\frac{5}{6}$    **b.** $\frac{4}{6}$ ◯ $\frac{1}{6}$    **c.** $\frac{3}{6}$ ◯ $\frac{6}{6}$    **d.** $\frac{5}{6}$ ◯ $\frac{4}{6}$

0                                                          1

**Preparing for Module 10**

Use these three numbers to write three different equations with the same total. Use each number once in each equation.

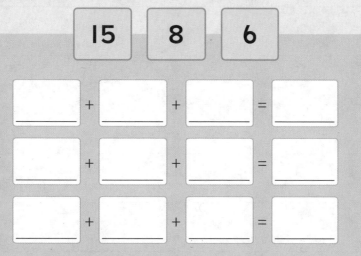

| 15 | 8 | 6 |

[____] + [____] + [____] = [____]

[____] + [____] + [____] = [____]

[____] + [____] + [____] = [____]

**Step In**

How could you measure the amount of surface a sheet of paper covers?

You could cover the sheet of paper with tiles, then count the tiles.

Which of these types of tiles would you use? Why?

Use an inch ruler to measure each side of an orange pattern block.

How long is each side? What shape is the block?

What is the area of the surface that the block covers?

The amount of surface that an item covers is called area.

It covers one square inch of surface. A square inch is a unit of area.

**Step Up**

1.  Use orange pattern blocks to cover the rectangle with no overlaps and without leaving gaps. Count the blocks then write the area.

Area is _____ square inches

**2.** Use a ruler to help you split each rectangle into square inches.
Count the number of square inches. Then write the area.

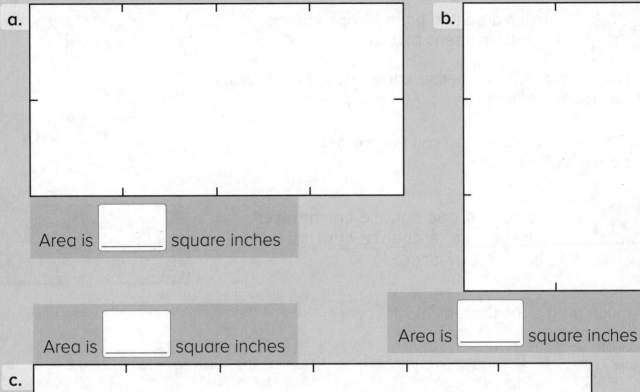

a.

Area is _____ square inches

b.

Area is _____ square inches

Area is _____ square inches

c.

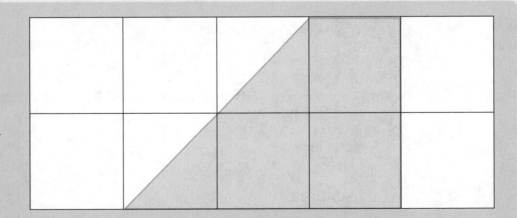

**Step Ahead**

Figure out the area of the orange quadrilateral.

Area is _____ square inches

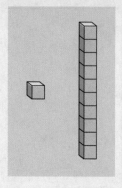

### Step In

Trace around a base-10 ones block and then a tens block.

Use a centimeter ruler to measure the sides of each block. Write the measurements on your tracings.

**What unit of area would you call the surface that the ones block covers?**

It covers one square centimeter of surface. A square centimeter is a unit of area.

A short way to write square centimeter is **sq cm**.

How much area does the tens block cover?

### Step Up

1. Use base-10 ones blocks to cover each rectangle with no overlaps and without leaving gaps. Write the area.

**A**

Area is _____ square cm

**B**

Area is _____ square cm

**C**

Area is _____ square cm

**D**

Area is _____ square cm

**E**

Area is _____ square cm

© ORIGO Education

**2. a.** In this grid, each square has an area of one square centimeter. Use the grid lines to draw three different rectangles.

**b.** In each rectangle you drew, write the area in square centimeters (sq cm).

**c.** Write **G** inside the rectangle with the **greatest** area.

**d.** Write **L** inside the rectangle with the **least** area.

**Step Ahead**

**a.** Measure the area of this rectangle using these blocks and write the number of each.

_____ orange pattern blocks _____ base-10 ones blocks

**b.** What do you notice?

**c.** Why do you think this happened?

**Computation Practice**     Why do some bulls wear bells?

★ Complete the equations. Then write each letter above its matching difference at the bottom of the page. Some letters appear more than once.

150 − 37 = ☐☐☐   **c**

285 − 68 = ☐☐☐   **r**

160 − 49 = ☐☐☐   **b**

464 − 48 = ☐☐☐   **u**

376 − 37 = ☐☐☐   **o**

270 − 58 = ☐☐☐   **k**

179 − 54 = ☐☐☐   **d**

152 − 46 = ☐☐☐   **w**

576 − 43 = ☐☐☐   **s**

154 − 36 = ☐☐☐   **t**

295 − 63 = ☐☐☐   **a**

687 − 64 = ☐☐☐   **e**

192 − 88 = ☐☐☐   **i**

182 − 79 = ☐☐☐   **n**

267 − 39 = ☐☐☐   **h**

| ☐ | ☐ | ☐ | ☐ | ☐ | ☐ | ☐ | | ☐ | ☐ | ☐ | ☐ | ☐ |
| 111 | 623 | 113 | 232 | 416 | 533 | 623 | | 118 | 228 | 623 | 104 | 217 |

| ☐ | ☐ | ☐ | ☐ | ☐ | | ☐ | ☐ | ☐ | ☐ |
| 228 | 339 | 217 | 103 | 533 | | 125 | 339 | 103 | 118 |

| ☐ | ☐ | ☐ | ☐ |
| 106 | 339 | 217 | 212 |

## Ongoing Practice

**1.** Color an array to match the numbers given.
Then complete the matching fact family.

**a.**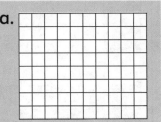

8 × 4 = ____

____ × ____ = ____

____ ÷ ____ = ____

____ ÷ ____ = ____

**b.**

5 × 8 = ____

____ × ____ = ____

____ ÷ ____ = ____

____ ÷ ____ = ____

**c.**

8 × 6 = ____

____ × ____ = ____

____ ÷ ____ = ____

____ ÷ ____ = ____

**d.**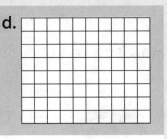

7 × 8 = ____

____ × ____ = ____

____ ÷ ____ = ____

____ ÷ ____ = ____

**2.** Use ones blocks to cover each rectangle without leaving gaps. Write the area.

**A**

Area _____ sq cm

**B**

Area _____ sq cm

**C**

Area _____ sq cm

## Preparing for Module 11

Look at the blocks. Write the matching number on the expander. Then write the number name.

thousands  hundreds

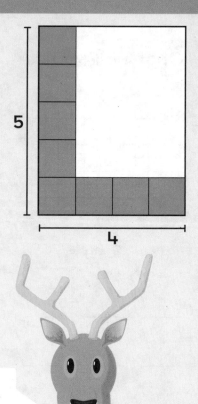

**Step In**

This picture shows that square tiles are being used to cover a floor.

How many tiles will be needed in total?

How can you use multiplication to quickly figure it out?

There are 5 rows and each row will have 4 squares.
5 × 4 = 20 so 20 tiles will be needed.

What is the area of the whole floor? How do you know?

5 × 4 = 20, so the area is 20 square units.

**Step Up**

1. Use multiplication to help you calculate the total area of each large rectangle.

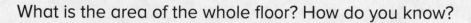

**a.**

Area is _____ sq units

**b.**

Area is _____ sq units

**c.**

Area is _____ sq units

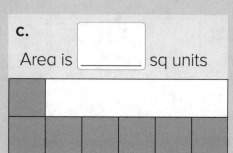

**d.**

Area is _____ sq units

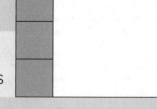

**2.** For each of these, use the grid lines to draw a rectangle that matches the description. Then use multiplication to calculate the area.

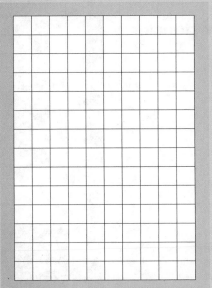

**a.** 8 units × 3 units

Area is _____ sq units

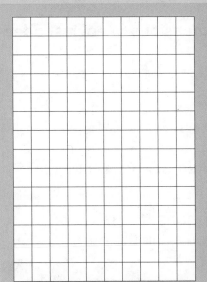

**b.** 4 units × 7 units

Area is _____ sq units

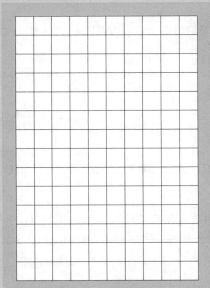

**c.** 6 units × 9 units

Area is _____ sq units

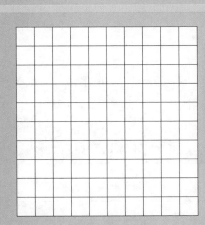

**d.** 7 units × 8 units

Area is _____ sq units

**e.** 5 units × 6 units

Area is _____ sq units

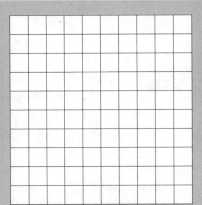

**Step Ahead**

Calculate the area of the red shape without counting every square. Show your thinking in the space below.

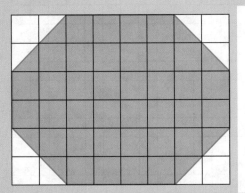

Area is _____ sq units

**Step In**    What are the dimensions of each shaded rectangle?

 ×  ×  ×

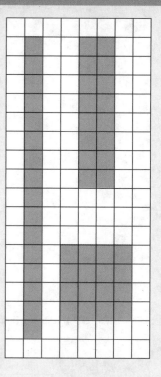

What do you notice about the area of each rectangle?

Olivia's rectangle has the dimensions 16 × 1.
If she flips the dimensions, do you think the area
of her rectangle will change?

**What could be the dimensions of a rectangle that has
an area of 8 square units?**

How can you figure it out?

**Step Up**    1.  Draw as many different rectangles as possible to match each area.
Write the dimensions beside each rectangle.

| a. | Area is 12 sq units |
| --- | --- |

| b. | Area is 18 sq units |
| --- | --- |

**2.** Write two different pairs of dimensions that will each give the same area.

**a.** Area is
15 sq units

**b.** Area is
32 sq units

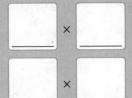

**c.** Area is
24 sq units

**d.** Area is
20 sq units

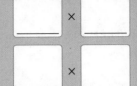

**3. a.** Circle one pair of dimensions from **each** area in Question 2.

    **b.** Draw a rectangle to match each pair of dimensions that you circled.
Label each rectangle you draw.

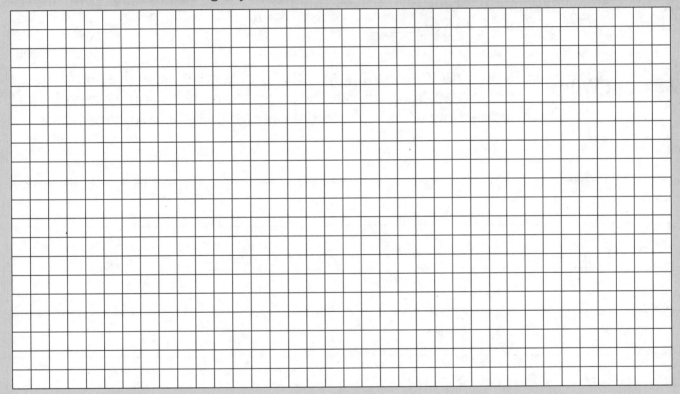

**Step Ahead**

Use the grid to help solve this problem. A garden in a park is shaped like a rectangle. It has an area of 60 square units. The longer side of the garden is 15 units long. How long is the shorter side?

_____ units long

## Think and Solve

Vincent can move one shape to make the number of kilograms on each scale the same.

**a.** Which shape can he move?

**b.** Where can he move it?

**c.** How many kilograms will be on each scale after the move?  kg

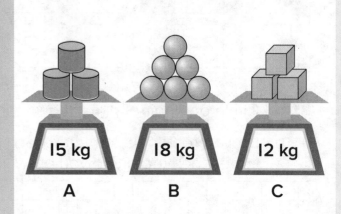

15 kg    18 kg    12 kg
 A        B        C

## Words at Work

Find a rectangular floor or wall that is covered with square tiles. It could be at home, at school, or somewhere you visit. Write in words how you calculate the area of the whole floor or wall.

**I.** Complete the multiplication fact that you could use to figure out the division fact. Then complete the division fact.

**a.**

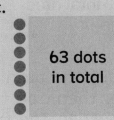

27 dots in total

$3 \times \underline{\hspace{1cm}} = 27$

$27 \div 3 = \underline{\hspace{1cm}}$

**b.**

45 dots in total

$\underline{\hspace{1cm}} \times 9 = 45$

$45 \div 9 = \underline{\hspace{1cm}}$

**c.**

63 dots in total

$7 \times \underline{\hspace{1cm}} = 63$

$63 \div 7 = \underline{\hspace{1cm}}$

**d.**

72 dots in total

$\underline{\hspace{1cm}} \times 9 = 72$

$72 \div 9 = \underline{\hspace{1cm}}$

**2.** Use multiplication to calculate the total area of each large rectangle.

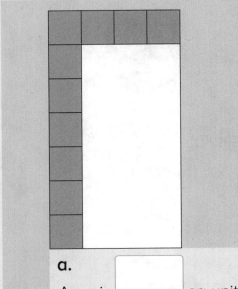

**a.**
Area is _____ sq units

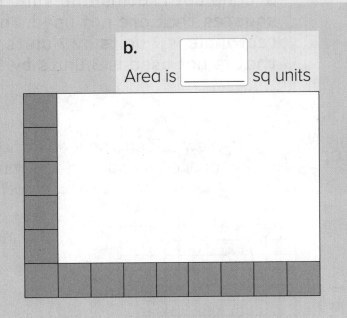

**b.**
Area is _____ sq units

Write each numeral in expanded form.

**a.** 5,467 _____

**b.** 1,908 _____

**c.** 4,096 _____

## Step In

This is a floor plan of part of a house.

How could you calculate the total area of the family room and kitchen?

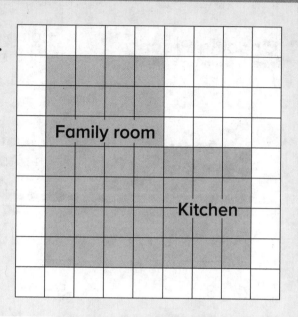

Family room

Kitchen

I would split the plan into two rooms then add the totals together. The family room is 7 units by 4 units. The kitchen is 4 units by 3 units.

I would start with a larger rectangle around both rooms and subtract the squares that are not used. The larger rectangle is 7 units by 7 units. The space that is not used is 3 units by 3 units.

## Step Up

I. New carpet is needed in these rooms. Calculate the area of each floor plan. Show your thinking.

a.

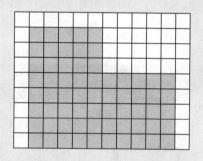

Area is _____ sq units

b.

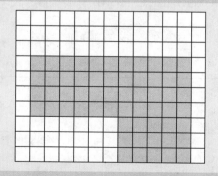

Area is _____ sq units

**2.** Calculate the area of each shaded shape. Show your thinking.

**a.**

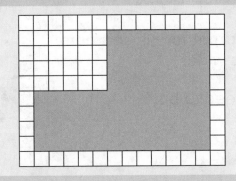

Area is _____ sq units

**b.**

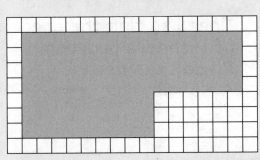

Area is _____ sq units

**3.** Draw floor plans like those in Question 2. Then write the area of each.

**a.** Less than 100 squares

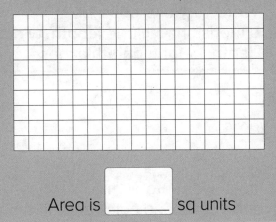

Area is _____ sq units

**b.** Less than 100 squares

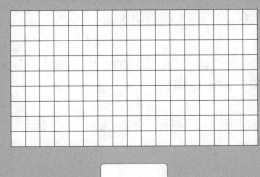

Area is _____ sq units

**Step Ahead**

Draw a floor plan with at least two rooms and a total area of about 75 square units.

Make sure you label each room.

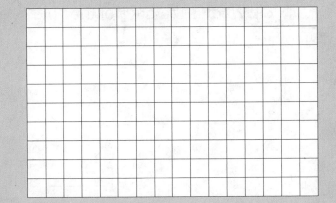

**Step In**  Michael's parents are buying new carpet for his bedroom. His floor is 5 yards long and 3 yards wide.

How many square yards of carpet will his parents need to buy?

Draw a picture to match the story.

> I need to find the area of Michael's bedroom. I'll call the area **A**.
> A = 5 × 3

**Dimensions tell you about distance.**
One dimension is **length**. Another dimension is **width**.

What are the dimensions of the floor in Michael's bedroom?

What words would you use to describe the dimensions of a wall?

> Words used to describe dimensions include **length**, **width**, **depth**, **height**, and **thickness**.

What abbreviations do you know for these measurement units?

| centimeters | meters | feet | yards |

**Step Up**  I.  Draw a simple picture to match each word problem. Then label the dimensions on your picture and calculate the area.

**a.**  A hallway is 9 feet long and 3 feet wide. The walls are 8 feet tall. What is the area of the floor?

Area _____ sq ft

**b.**  A garden has 9 tomato plants in it. The garden is 2 meters by 7 meters. What is the area of the garden?

Area _____ sq m

**2.** Read the problems and answer the questions.

**a.** Carmela estimates that the paint she has will cover 40 square feet. She has to paint a wall that is 8 feet high and 6 feet long.

What is the area of the wall she has to paint? [_____] sq ft

Will she have enough paint? [_____]

**b.** Alexis's garden is 6 meters by 3 meters. She buys a bag of fertilizer that can be spread over 50 square meters.

What is the area of the garden? [_____] sq m

Will she have enough fertilizer? [_____]

**3.** Complete the equation to match the word problem. Then write the area.

**a.** A bulletin board is 3 feet wide and 4 feet long. It has 8 notices on it. What is its area?

A = [_____]

Area [_____] sq ft

**b.** A trailer is 5 feet wide and 8 feet long. It is holding 10 large boxes. What is its area?

A = [_____]

Area [_____] sq ft

**c.** A tent measures 8 feet by 7 feet. It fits 4 people. What is its area?

A = [_____]

Area [_____] sq ft

**d.** A solar panel costs $400 and measures 5 feet by 3 feet. What is its area?

A = [_____]

Area [_____] sq ft

---

**Step Ahead**

Write an area word problem to match this equation. Then write the area.

A = 4 cm × 7 cm

[_____]

[_____]

[_____]

## Computation Practice

★ For each of these, write the the product and then write
the turnaround fact. Use the classroom clock to time yourself.

**Time Taken:**

**start**

$9 \times 1 = $ ☐

☐ $\times$ ☐ $=$ ☐

$7 \times 9 = $ ☐

☐ $\times$ ☐ $=$ ☐

$5 \times 6 = $ ☐

☐ $\times$ ☐ $=$ ☐

$6 \times 8 = $ ☐

☐ $\times$ ☐ $=$ ☐

$2 \times 6 = $ ☐

☐ $\times$ ☐ $=$ ☐

$8 \times 9 = $ ☐

☐ $\times$ ☐ $=$ ☐

$6 \times 3 = $ ☐

☐ $\times$ ☐ $=$ ☐

$6 \times 0 = $ ☐

☐ $\times$ ☐ $=$ ☐

$9 \times 2 = $ ☐

☐ $\times$ ☐ $=$ ☐

$4 \times 6 = $ ☐

☐ $\times$ ☐ $=$ ☐

$4 \times 9 = $ ☐

☐ $\times$ ☐ $=$ ☐

$10 \times 9 = $ ☐

☐ $\times$ ☐ $=$ ☐

$9 \times 1 = $ ☐

☐ $\times$ ☐ $=$ ☐

$1 \times 6 = $ ☐

☐ $\times$ ☐ $=$ ☐

**finish**

$6 \times 9 = $ ☐

☐ $\times$ ☐ $=$ ☐

$9 \times 3 = $ ☐

☐ $\times$ ☐ $=$ ☐

$0 \times 9 = $ ☐

☐ $\times$ ☐ $=$ ☐

1. Color an array to match the numbers given. Then complete the fact family to match.

a.

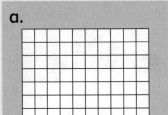

$4 \times 9 =$ _____

___ × ___ = ___

___ ÷ ___ = ___

___ ÷ ___ = ___

b.

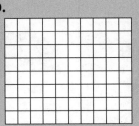

$7 \times 9 =$ _____

___ × ___ = ___

___ ÷ ___ = ___

___ ÷ ___ = ___

c.

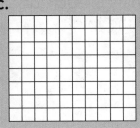

$3 \times 9 =$ _____

___ × ___ = ___

___ ÷ ___ = ___

___ ÷ ___ = ___

d.

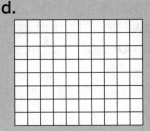

$5 \times 9 =$ _____

___ × ___ = ___

___ ÷ ___ = ___

___ ÷ ___ = ___

FROM 3.8.2

2. Calculate the area of the shaded shape. Show your thinking.

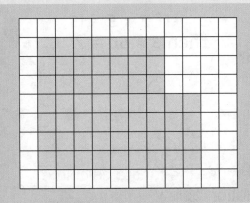

Area [_____] sq units

FROM 3.10.5

Round each number to the nearest **ten**, then the nearest **hundred**.

| Number | Nearest ten | Nearest hundred |
|---|---|---|
| 3,647 | | |
| 6,995 | | |
| 5,437 | | |

**Step In**

What multiplication sentence could you write to match this picture?

Imagine you had 20 marbles in each jar. How could you calculate the total number of marbles?

20 is ten times as many as 2, so the answer will be 10 times as many.

If 4 × 2 = 8
then 4 × 20 = 80

**What multiplication fact could you write to match this array?**

Imagine there were 50 dots in each row. How would the total number of dots change?

What multiplication equation could you write to match?

If 3 × 5 = 15
then 3 × 50 = ?

**Step Up**

1. Complete the multiplication fact. Then use the fact to calculate the product in the multiplication equation below.

a.
If 6 × 2 = _____

then 6 × 20 = _____

b.
If 4 × 5 = _____

then 4 × 50 = _____

c.
If 2 × 8 = _____

then 2 × 80 = _____

d.
If 7 × 4 = _____

then 7 × 40 = _____

e.
If 5 × 9 = _____

then 5 × 90 = _____

f.
If 4 × 3 = _____

then 4 × 30 = _____

**2.** Write the missing product.
Then write the related multiplication fact you used to figure it out.

**a.**
7 × 20 = _____

_____ × _____ = _____

**b.**
5 × 60 = _____

_____ × _____ = _____

**c.**
2 × 90 = _____

_____ × _____ = _____

**d.**
80 × 4 = _____

_____ × _____ = _____

**e.**
70 × 5 = _____

_____ × _____ = _____

**f.**
50 × 5 = _____

_____ × _____ = _____

**3.** Write an equation to show each problem. Be sure to include the product.

**a.** There are 60 blocks in each box. There are 4 boxes. How many blocks are there in total?

_____

**b.** There are 20 bars in each pack. There are 8 packs in a box. What is the total number of bars in one box?

_____

**c.** There are 5 pieces of string. Each piece is 90 cm long. What is the total length of string?

_____

**d.** There are 70 students in Grade 3. Each student has 4 counters. How many counters are there in total?

_____

**Step Ahead**

The shaded squares show 7 × 2. Shade or outline more squares onto the example shown to show 7 × 20.

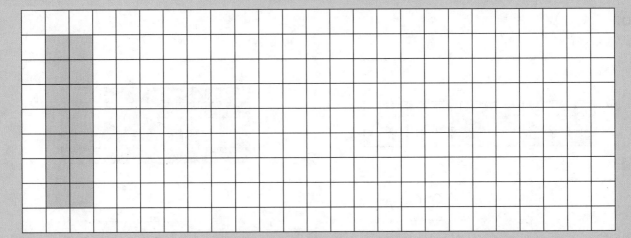

**Step In**   Felix is painting the concrete floor of a warehouse.

He needs to know the area of the floor
to calculate how much paint to buy.
The dimensions are shown to the right.

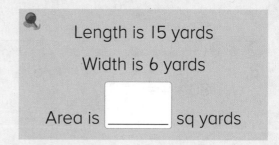

Length is 15 yards

Width is 6 yards

Area is _____ sq yards

Estimate the area of the floor.
Would it be more or less than 100 sq yards?

How could you calculate the exact area?

Hassun drew this grid to help. He split 15 into tens and ones
then multiplied 6 × 10 and 6 × 5.

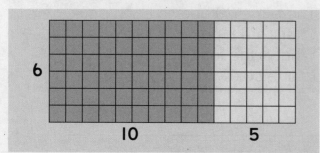

6

10    5

You can split a rectangle
into parts to find the
**partial products.**

How could you use this strategy to calculate 3 × 28?

*3 × 20 is 60 and 3 × 8 is 24. I then put these
partial products together to calculate the total.*

**Step Up**

I.   Write the product for each part. Then write the total.
     Make an estimate to check each total.

**a.**

3 × 10 = _____        3 × 6 = _____

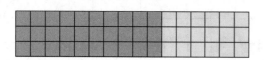

3 × 16 = _____

**b.**

5 × 10 = _____        5 × 3 = _____

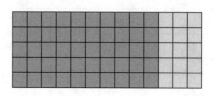

5 × 13 = _____

**2.** Draw a line to split each rectangle into parts that are easy for you to multiply. Then calculate the area. Make an estimate to check each area.

**a.**

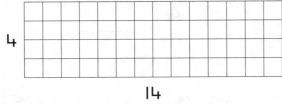

4

14

Area _____ sq units

**b.**

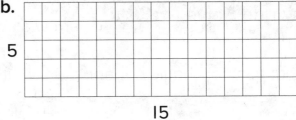

5

15

Area _____ sq units

**c.**

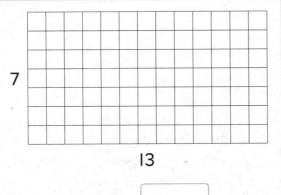

7

13

Area _____ sq units

**d.**

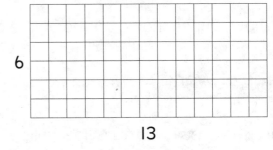

6

13

Area _____ sq units

**e.**

5

23

Area _____ sq units

**Step Ahead**

Zoe's garden is 19 feet long and 5 feet wide. Draw and label a picture to help you calculate the area of her garden.

_____ sq ft

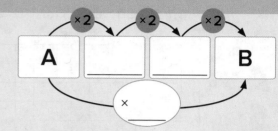

**Think and Solve**  Look at this arrow diagram.

**1.** What number should appear in Box B, if

**a.**

5 is placed in Box A? _____

**b.**

8 is placed in Box A? _____

**c.**

3 is placed in Box A? _____

**d.**

10 is placed in Box A? _____

**2.** What number should appear in the oval? _____

**Words at Work**   Write in words how you solve this problem.

Mr. Tran is painting his office walls. One of the walls is completely made of glass so it does not need to be painted. He will apply two coats of paint to make sure the old paint is covered well. Each wall is 12 feet long and 8 feet high. The paint comes in cans. Each can covers about 400 square feet. How many cans will he need to completely paint the walls?

**Ongoing Practice**

1. Complete these standard addition algorithms.

a.
| H | T | O |
|---|---|---|
| 3 | 5 | 2 |
| + 1 | 3 | 6 |

b.
| H | T | O |
|---|---|---|
| 4 | 3 | 7 |
| + | 5 | 6 |

c.
| H | T | O |
|---|---|---|
| 2 | 8 | 3 |
| + | 7 | 6 |

d.
| H | T | O |
|---|---|---|
| 3 | 6 | 5 |
| + 2 | 0 | 8 |

2. Complete the number fact. Then use the fact to calculate the product below.

a.
If 5 × 3 = _____

Then 5 × 30 = _____

b.
If 3 × 4 = _____

Then 3 × 40 = _____

c.
If 2 × 7 = _____

Then 2 × 70 = _____

d.
If 6 × 5 = _____

Then 6 × 50 = _____

e.
If 9 × 2 = _____

Then 9 × 20 = _____

f.
If 4 × 8 = _____

Then 4 × 80 = _____

**Preparing for Module 11**    Write the total amount of money.

a.

The total is $_____ and _____¢

b.

The total is $_____ and _____¢

## Step In    How could you calculate the number of squares in this array?

Imagine the array is cut in half and the new array below is made. with the two pieces.

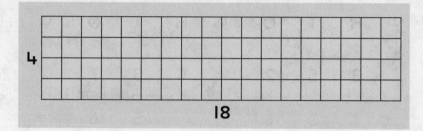

What is different about the arrays?

Has the number of squares changed?

Is it easier to calculate the total number of squares for the new array? Why?

Write an equation to describe each array.

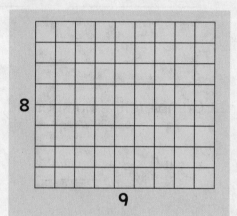

Doubling one number and halving the other can make it easier to figure out the product.

## Step Up

I. Imagine this array was cut in half and rearranged.
Color squares in the **after** picture to show the new array.
Label the dimensions then complete the equations.

**Before**

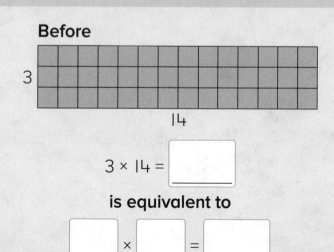

3 × 14 = ☐

**is equivalent to**

☐ × ☐ = ☐

**After**

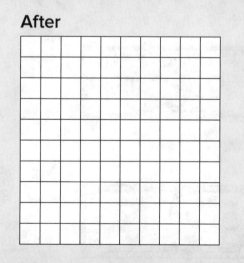

**2.** Double one number and halve the other. Then write the products.

**a.**

$3 \times 16 = $ ☐

is equal to

___ × ___ = ___

**b.**

$4 \times 14 = $ ☐

is equal to

___ × ___ = ___

**c.**

$5 \times 16 = $ ☐

is equal to

___ × ___ = ___

**d.**

$15 \times 6 = $ ☐

is equal to

___ × ___ = ___

**e.**

$4 \times 15 = $ ☐

is equal to

___ × ___ = ___

**f.**

$18 \times 5 = $ ☐

is equal to

___ × ___ = ___

**3. a.** Circle all the equations that you would solve by doubling one number and halving the other.

$25 \times 7 = ?$    $15 \times 6 = ?$    $25 \times 9 = ?$    $17 \times 5 = ?$    $16 \times 4 = ?$    $8 \times 15 = ?$

**b.** Look carefully at the numbers you circled. Are the numbers odd, even, or odd and even? Write what you notice.

---

**Step Ahead**

**a.** Claire wants to use the double-and-halve strategy to solve this problem. Explain why this strategy is **not** the best one to use.

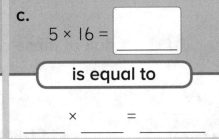

$5 \times 13 = ?$

**b.** Suggest a different strategy that she could choose.

**Step In**   Look at these comic books.

A   **ACTION COMICS** $9 an issue

B  **SPACE ADVENTURE** $7 an issue

C  **DINO STORIE** $6 an issue

D  **DETECTIVE MYSTERY** ?? $8 an issue

Imagine you want to buy one issue of **A** and three issues of **B**.

What steps would you use to calculate the total cost?

What equation could you write to show your thinking?

These are the rules for the order of operations.

If there is **one** type of operation in a sentence, work left to right.

If there is **more than one** type of operation, work left to right in this order.
1. perform any operation inside parentheses
2. multiply or divide pairs of numbers
3. add or subtract pairs of numbers

Imagine you want to buy three issues of **C** and two issues of **D**.

Working left to right, what is the total cost?
Using the order of multiple operations, what total do you get?

What do you notice?

$3 \times 6 + 2 \times 8 =$ _____

18 + 16

**Step Up**   1. Use the comic book prices above. Write an equation to show how you would calculate the total cost for each purchase. Then write the total.

a. Buy five **C** and one **A** _____

b. Buy two **B** and one **D** _____

**2.** Use the comic book prices at the top of page 384.
Write an equation to show how you calculate the total cost of each purchase.
Write the products in each box to help.

**a.**

Buy 5 **A** and 2 **B**

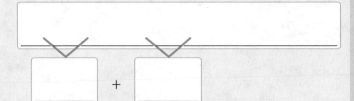

$5 \times 9$ + $2 \times 7$ = ____

____ + ____

**b.**

Buy 2 **B** and 3 **A**

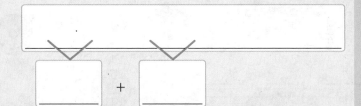

____ + ____

**c.**

Buy 3 **D** and 3 **C**

____

____ + ____

**3.** Write a word problem to match this equation.   $4 \times 3 + 8 = ?$

_____

_____

_____

**Step Ahead**   Tyler calculates the total cost of 3 child meals and 2 adult meals.
He thinks: $3 \times 8 + 2 \times 10$ and gets a total of $260.

**MEAL DEAL**

| Child | $8 |
| Adult | $10 |

**a.** The correct total is  $ _____ .

**b.** Describe his mistake in words.

_____

_____

**Computation Practice**     What twists and turns around America but never moves?

★ Write a multiplication fact you can use to figure out each division fact. Then write the quotients. Use a ruler to draw a straight line from each quotient on the left to a matching quotient on the right. The line will pass through a number and a letter. Write each letter above its matching number at the bottom of the page.

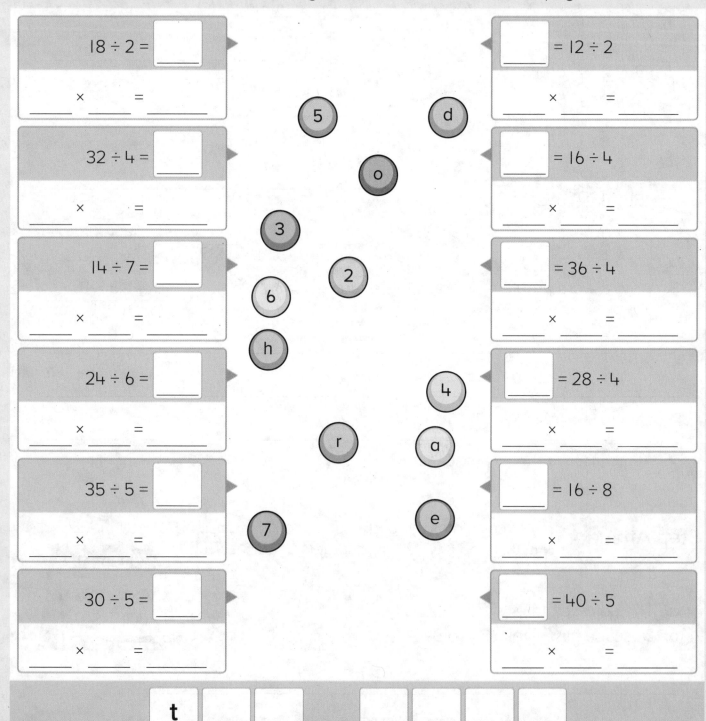

18 ÷ 2 = ☐      ___ × ___ = ___

32 ÷ 4 = ☐      ___ × ___ = ___

14 ÷ 7 = ☐      ___ × ___ = ___

24 ÷ 6 = ☐      ___ × ___ = ___

35 ÷ 5 = ☐      ___ × ___ = ___

30 ÷ 5 = ☐      ___ × ___ = ___

☐ = 12 ÷ 2      ___ × ___ = ___

☐ = 16 ÷ 4      ___ × ___ = ___

☐ = 36 ÷ 4      ___ × ___ = ___

☐ = 28 ÷ 4      ___ × ___ = ___

☐ = 16 ÷ 8      ___ × ___ = ___

☐ = 40 ÷ 5      ___ × ___ = ___

5   d   o   3   2   6   h   4   r   a   7   e

t ☐ ☐   ☐ ☐ ☐ ☐
  2 3   4 5 6 7

## Ongoing Practice

**I.** Complete these standard algorithms.

**a.**

| H | T | O |
|---|---|---|
| 6 | 4 | 1 |
| + 1 | 8 | 5 |

**b.**

| H | T | O |
|---|---|---|
| 3 | 5 | 6 |
| + 4 | 7 | 8 |

**c.**

| H | T | O |
|---|---|---|
| 5 | 3 | 8 |
| + 2 | 9 | 3 |

**2.** Write the product in the first equation. Then write the related multiplication fact you used to figure it out.

**a.**

$2 \times 40 =$ _____

_____ $\times$ _____ $=$ _____

**b.**

$4 \times 50 =$ _____

_____ $\times$ _____ $=$ _____

**c.**

$70 \times 2 =$ _____

_____ $\times$ _____ $=$ _____

**d.**

$20 \times 8 =$ _____

_____ $\times$ _____ $=$ _____

**e.**

$30 \times 5 =$ _____

_____ $\times$ _____ $=$ _____

**f.**

$40 \times 6 =$ _____

_____ $\times$ _____ $=$ _____

## Preparing for Module II

Use tallies to show how to pay for the item using **each** of the bills shown. Use amounts that will give you just a few dollars in change.

**I.**

 $28

**a.**

**b.**

**2.**

 $64

**a.**

**b.**

**Step In**

Daniel has **$16** and buys one of each meal deal.
How much money does he have left?

Deal A
$4

WATER

Deal B
$7

Tama wrote this equation to figure it out.

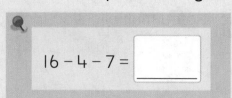

$16 - 4 - 7 = \boxed{\phantom{00}}$

Emilia wrote this equation.

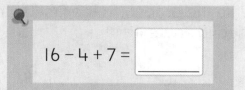

$16 - 4 + 7 = \boxed{\phantom{00}}$

What answer will they each have?

What do you notice?

What should Emilia do to make it clear that
the 4 and 7 must be added first?

Parentheses help make it clear what to do first
or what parts of the sentence should be done
together. I want to add the 4 and 7 first, so
I'll write 16 - (4 + 7). The answer is 5.

**Step Up**

1. Calculate the part in the parentheses and write the new problem.
   Then write the answer.

a.
$15 + (8 \times 5)$

$\underline{15} + \underline{40}$

$\underline{55}$

Answer is $\underline{55}$

b.
$(20 + 8) \div 4$

$\underline{\phantom{00}} \div \underline{\phantom{00}}$

Answer is $\underline{\phantom{00}}$

c.
$5 \times (9 - 2)$

$\underline{\phantom{00}} \times \underline{\phantom{00}}$

Answer is $\underline{\phantom{00}}$

**2.** Complete each of these. Follow the steps used in Question 1 on page 388.

**a.**

$(21 - 5) \div 8$

_____

Answer is _____

**b.**

$9 \times (4 + 5)$

_____

Answer is _____

**c.**

$56 - (60 \div 6)$

_____

Answer is _____

**d.**

$20 - (40 \div 5)$

_____

Answer is _____

**e.**

$100 + (8 \times 7)$

_____

Answer is _____

**f.**

$37 + (8 \div 2)$

_____

Answer is _____

**3.** Complete each equation.

**a.**
$6 \times (7 + 3) = \boxed{\phantom{000}}$

**b.**
$40 - (15 + 16) = \boxed{\phantom{000}}$

**c.**
$6 \times (9 \div 9) = \boxed{\phantom{000}}$

**d.**
$(8 + 4) \times 2 = \boxed{\phantom{000}}$

**e.**
$36 \div (3 \times 2) = \boxed{\phantom{000}}$

**f.**
$(7 - 7) \times 6 = \boxed{\phantom{000}}$

**Step Ahead**  Color the ⬭ beside the thinking you could use to solve each problem.

**a.**
Dallas had $35. She bought 4 cups that cost $3 each. How much money does she have left?

- ⬭ $35 - (4 \times 3)$
- ⬭ $(35 - 4) \times 3$
- ⬭ $4 \times 3 - 35$

**b.**
6 star stickers and 10 smiley face stickers were shared equally among 8 children. How many stickers did each child get?

- ⬭ $8 \div 6 + 10$
- ⬭ $(6 + 10) \div 8$
- ⬭ $(6 + 10) - 8$

**c.**
Beatrice buys 8 shirts that cost $8 each. How much change does she get from $100?

- ⬭ $(8 \times 8) - 100$
- ⬭ $100 - (8 + 8)$
- ⬭ $100 - (8 \times 8)$

**Step In**

Ashley bought 3 figurines that cost **$6** each.
She paid with a **$20** bill.

How much change should she receive?

What equation could you write to show your thinking?

Gabriel wrote this equation to calculate the change.

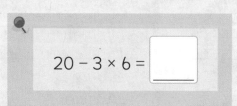

$$20 - 3 \times 6 = \boxed{\phantom{00}}$$

○ $6 each

What part of the equation should you do first? How do you know?

Why are parentheses not needed in Gabriel's equation?

Could you use them anyway?

You don't have to use parentheses,
but they can make things clearer.

**Step Up**

1. Read the word problem. Then color the ○ beside the thinking
you would use to calculate the answer.

**a.**
Aston had $40.
He bought 4 tickets that cost $7 each.
How much money does he have left?

- ○ $40 - 4 \times 7$
- ○ $(40 - 4) \times 7$
- ○ $4 \times 7 - 40$

**b.**
9 apples and 3 bananas were shared
equally among 6 children.
How many pieces of fruit were in each share?

- ○ $9 + 3 \div 6$
- ○ $(9 + 3) \div 6$
- ○ $(9 + 3) - 6$

**c.**
The coach bought 9 shirts that cost $7 each.
How much change did she get from $100?

- ○ $(9 \times 7) - 100$
- ○ $100 - (9 + 7)$
- ○ $100 - (9 \times 7)$

**2.** Write how you would solve each problem. Then write the answer.

**a.** Grace had $25. Then she and 3 friends equally shared a raffle prize of $60. How much money does Grace have now?

**b.** Fiona had $24 in her purse. She spent $19, then withdrew $20 from an ATM to pay for an $8 lunch. How much money does she have left in her purse?

**c.** Owen earned $8 each week for 6 weeks. He then bought a game for $37. How much money does he have left?

**d.** Charlotte had $18 and then earned $17 more. She bought 3 books for $5 each. How much money does she have left?

**e.** A family pass for 4 people costs $35. How much cheaper is the family pass than paying $12 for each ticket?

**f.** Teena, Allan, and Hugo split $36 equally. Hugo then spent $7 of his share. How much money does he have left?

**Step Ahead**

Write a word problem that uses more than one operation. Then exchange problems with another student and have them write an equation to match.

### Think and Solve  THINK TANK

Draw lines **inside** this rectangle to make
3 smaller rectangles that are the **same** size.
Write the length and width of the smaller rectangles.

18 cm

3 cm

### Words at Work

Write a word problem that involves subtraction and multiplication.
Then write how you find the solution.

## Ongoing Practice

**1.** Complete these standard addition algorithms.

**a.**

| H | T | O |
|---|---|---|
|   | 6 | 7 |
| + | 1 | 8 |
|   |   |   |

**b.**

| H | T | O |
|---|---|---|
|   | 5 | 6 |
| + | 2 | 7 |
|   |   |   |

**c.**

| H | T | O |
|---|---|---|
| 2 | 7 | 6 |
| + | 5 | 5 |
|   |   |   |

**d.**

| H | T | O |
|---|---|---|
| 3 | 6 | 8 |
| + | 7 | 4 |
|   |   |   |

**e.**

| H | T | O |
|---|---|---|
| 1 | 4 | 6 |
| + 4 | 2 | 8 |
|   |   |   |

**f.**

| H | T | O |
|---|---|---|
| 3 | 7 | 3 |
| + 4 | 8 | 8 |
|   |   |   |

**2.** Double one number and halve the other. Then write the products.

**a.**
18 × 6 = _____

is equal to

_____ × _____ = _____

**b.**
6 × 15 = _____

is equal to

_____ × _____ = _____

**c.**
4 × 35 = _____

is equal to

_____ × _____ = _____

## Preparing for Module 11

Use red to circle the container that holds the **most**.
Use blue to circle the container that holds the **least**.

I pint

I cup

I quart

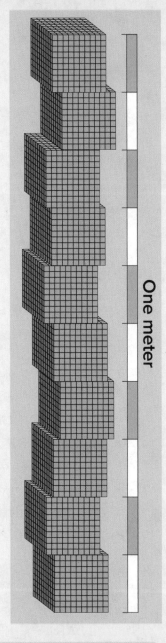

One meter

**Step In** — What number does one of these blocks represent?
How do you know?

What number is represented by 10 of these blocks?
How do you know?

How many **hundreds** blocks could you regroup
as 10 thousands blocks?

How many **tens** blocks could you regroup
as 10 thousands blocks?

How did you figure it out?

Write numbers on each expander to show the different ways
to describe the stack.

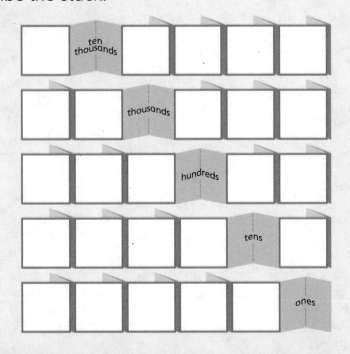

**Step Up** — 1. Look at the abacus. Write the matching number on the expander.

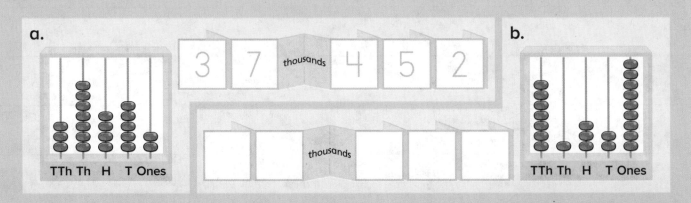

a.

TTh Th H T Ones

3 7 thousands 4 5 2

thousands

b.

TTh Th H T Ones

© ORIGO Education

**2.** Draw beads or write numbers to complete the missing parts.

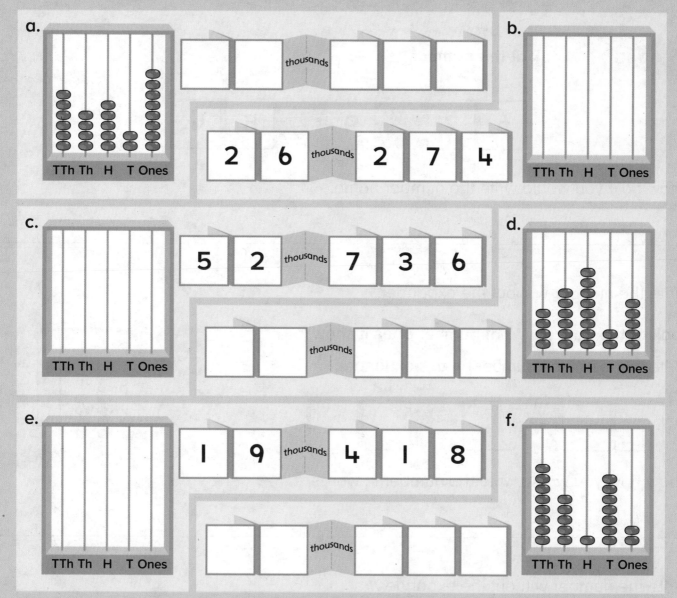

a.

TTh Th H T Ones

| 2 | 6 | thousands | 2 | 7 | 4 |

b.

TTh Th H T Ones

c.

| 5 | 2 | thousands | 7 | 3 | 6 |

TTh Th H T Ones

d.

TTh Th H T Ones

e.

| 1 | 9 | thousands | 4 | 1 | 8 |

TTh Th H T Ones

f.

TTh Th H T Ones

**Step Ahead**

Imagine you had only hundreds, tens, and ones blocks.
Write how you could represent this number.

| 7 | 5 | thousands | 2 | 5 | 3 |

**Step In**    Look at this number.

Show how you would write the number name.

Write the number without the expander.

**Look at the abacus. What number does it show?**

Write the matching number on this expander.

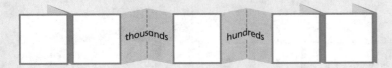

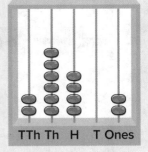

Show how you would write the number in words.

Write the number without the expander.

**Step Up**    1.  Draw beads on each abacus to represent the number.

a.    27,605

b.    60,035

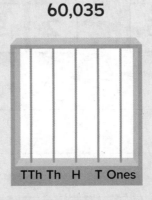

c.    43,070

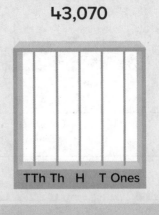

**2.** Complete the missing parts.

a.

| 9 | 7 | thousands | 6 | hundreds | 1 | 3 |

b.

| 6 | 2 | thousands | 4 | hundreds | 0 | 8 |

c.

| | | thousands | | hundreds | | |

fifty-one thousand four hundred twenty

d.

93,604

| | | thousands | | hundreds | | |

e.

35,072

| | | thousands | | hundreds | | |

**Step Ahead**

Draw beads on the abacus to represent a number that has **more hundreds than ones** and **no tens.** Then write your number in words.

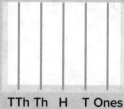

TTh Th H T Ones

**Computation Practice**

**What is the largest structure ever made by living creatures?**

★ Complete the equations. Then write each letter above its matching product at the bottom of the page.

| | | |
|---|---|---|
| $9 \times 8 =$ ___ **h** | $1 \times 9 =$ ___ **r** | $8 \times 7 =$ ___ **e** |
| $5 \times 9 =$ ___ **i** | $2 \times 9 =$ ___ **e** | $8 \times 3 =$ ___ **e** |
| $9 \times 9 =$ ___ **a** | $6 \times 5 =$ ___ **r** | $6 \times 9 =$ ___ **t** |
| $9 \times 4 =$ ___ **t** | $5 \times 8 =$ ___ **r** | $8 \times 2 =$ ___ **r** |
| $5 \times 5 =$ ___ **e** | $9 \times 0 =$ ___ **e** | $3 \times 9 =$ ___ **a** |
| $7 \times 4 =$ ___ **r** | $4 \times 8 =$ ___ **g** | $7 \times 9 =$ ___ **b** |
| $5 \times 7 =$ ___ **f** | | |

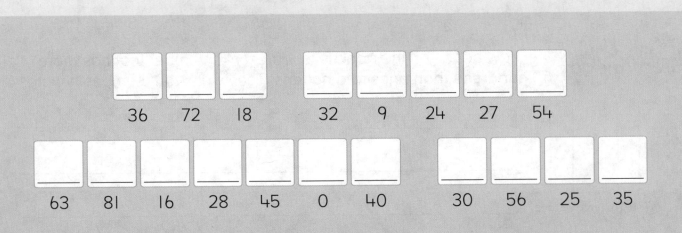

36   72   18       32   9   24   27   54

63   81   16   28   45   0   40       30   56   25   35

© ORIGO Education

1.  Write a word problem to match this equation. $6 \times 9 + 7 = ?$

FROM 3.9.12

2.  Draw beads or write numbers to complete the missing parts.

FROM 3.11.1

**a.**

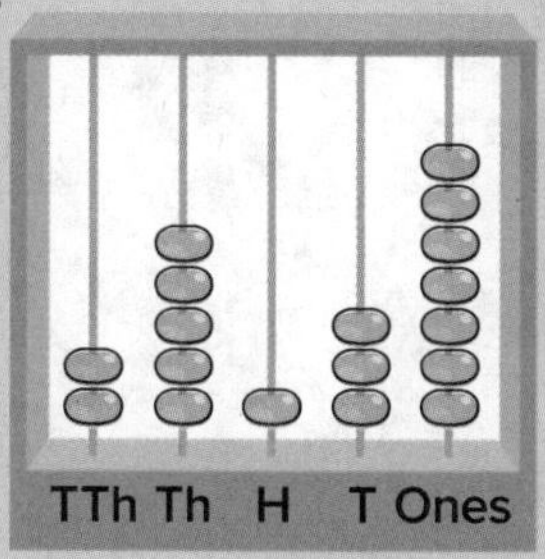

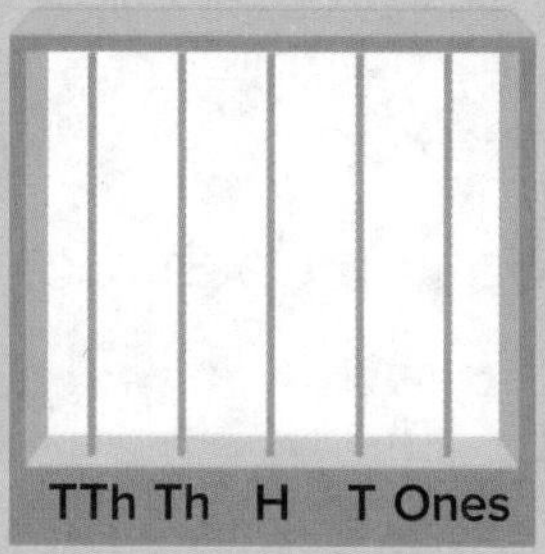

TTh  Th  H  T  Ones

| | | thousands | | | |

| 1 | 5 | thousands | 3 | 5 | 2 |

**b.**

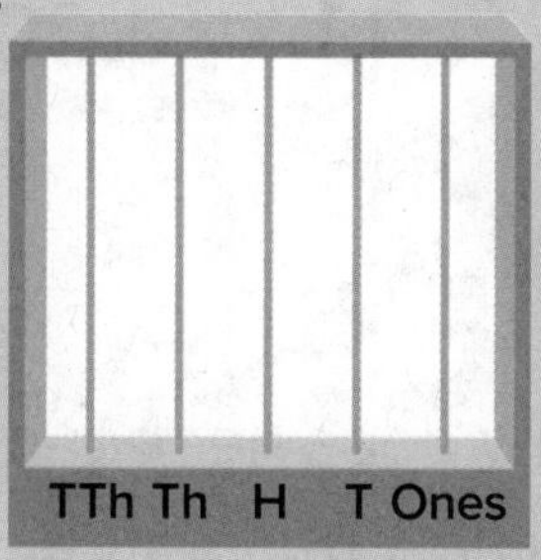

TTh  Th  H  T  Ones

**c.**

TTh  Th  H  T  Ones

| 4 | 1 | thousands | 2 | 0 | 8 |

| | | thousands | | | |

**d.**

TTh  Th  H  T  Ones

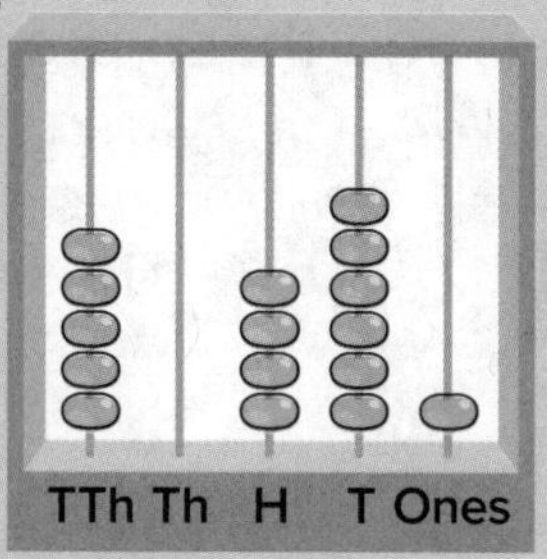

**Preparing for Module 12**    Write the missing numbers.

**a.**

Half of 4 is ____

**so**

Half of 40 is ____

**b.**

Half of 6 is ____

**so**

Half of 60 is ____

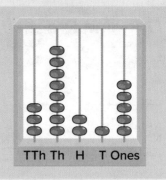

TTh Th H T Ones

**Step In**     What number is shown on this abacus?

Look at the rod that represents the ten-thousands place. How many beads can you see?

What number do the beads on that rod show?

> I can see 3 beads in the ten-thousands place. I know that each bead represents 10,000. So 3 × 10,000 = 30,000.

What number do the beads on each of the other place-value rods show?

Jennifer writes the number in **expanded form**.

**(3 × 10,000) + (8 × 1,000) + (2 × 100) + (1 × 10) + (5 × 1) = ?**

_____ + _____ + _____ + _____ + _____

How does her equation match the abacus?

Multiply the numbers inside each pair of parentheses. Record each product below the parentheses.

Now add these products. What do you notice?

**Step Up**     1.   Look at the abacus. Then write the value of the beads on each rod.

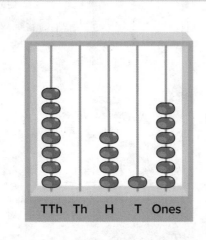

TTh Th H T Ones

_____ × 10,000 = _____

_____ × 1,000 = _____

_____ × 100 = _____

_____ × 10 = _____

_____ × 1 = _____

**2.** Write a five-digit number on each expander.
Then write the same number in expanded form.

**a.**

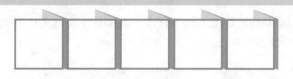

( _____ × 10,000) + ( _____ × 1,000) + ( _____ × 100) + ( _____ × 10) + ( _____ × 1)

**b.**

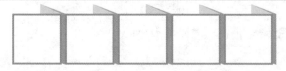

( _____ × 10,000) + ( _____ × 1,000) + ( _____ × 100) + ( _____ × 10) + ( _____ × 1)

**3.** Write each number in expanded form.

**a.**

22,418 _____

**b.**

16,789 _____

**c.**

79,533 _____

**d.**

40,210 _____

**Step Ahead**    Write the number that has been expanded.

**a.**

_____    (6 × 10,000) + (3 × 1,000) + (8 × 100) + (9 × 10)

**b.**

_____    (4 × 10,000) + (7 × 100) + (9 × 10) + (2 × 1)

**Step In**

This table shows the current seating capacities of ten stadiums in the United States.

| Stadium | Location | Seating Capacity |
|---|---|---|
| Memorial Stadium | Nebraska | 92,047 |
| Arrowhead Stadium | Missouri | 79,451 |
| Commonwealth Stadium | Kentucky | 67,606 |
| Sun Life Stadium | Florida | 74,916 |
| Kinnick Stadium | Iowa | 70,585 |
| Cotton Bowl | Texas | 92,100 |
| Notre Dame Stadium | Indiana | 80,795 |
| Folsom Field | Colorado | 53,750 |
| Sanford Stadium | Georgia | 92,746 |
| Jordan-Hare Stadium | Alabama | 87,451 |

How can you compare the seating capacities for the stadiums in Florida and Iowa?

What part of the numbers would you look at first?

Complete these relationship statements to describe the comparison.

| | **is less than** | |
|---|---|---|
| | **<** | |
| | **>** | |

**Step Up**

1. Look at the table above. Write the seating capacity of the stadiums in these locations. Then write **<** or **>** to make the statement true.

**a.** Colorado      Georgia

◯

**b.** Nebraska      Florida

◯

**c.** Missouri      Kentucky

◯

**d.** Colorado      Texas

◯

**2.** Use the data in the table at the top of page 404 to complete these.

**a.** Alabama _____ ◯ Missouri _____

**b.** Indiana _____ ◯ Iowa _____

**c.** Iowa _____ ◯ Missouri _____

**d.** Kentucky _____ ◯ Colorado _____

**e.** Texas _____ ◯ Georgia _____

**f.** Nebraska _____ ◯ Alabama _____

**3.** Look at the table on page 404. Follow the arrows to write the seating capacities in order from **least** to **greatest**.

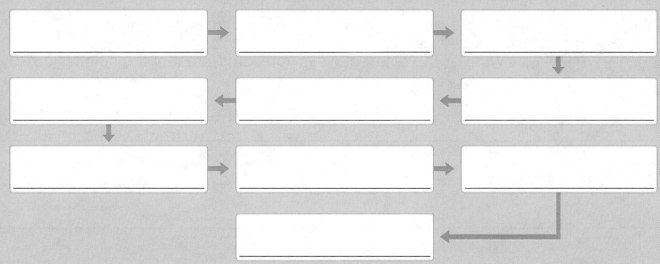

---

## Step Ahead

The Rose Bowl is in California.

It seats more people than the stadium in Texas but fewer people than the stadium in Georgia.

Color the ◯ beside the seating capacity of the Rose Bowl.

◯ 93,057     ◯ 92,098     ◯ 92,542

## Think and Solve

Read the directions first.

In the first circle, draw a line to make 2 parts the **same** size and shape.
The sum of the numbers in each part **must** be the **same**.
Then, in the second circle, draw a line in a different place to show another way.

## Words at Work

Write all the different ways you can represent the number 26,354.

## Ongoing Practice

**1.** Complete each equation.

**a.**
$(6 + 7) \times 2 =$ ☐

**b.**
$9 \times (12 \div 4) =$ ☐

**c.**
$20 - (8 + 4) =$ ☐

**d.**
$24 \div (4 \times 2) =$ ☐

**e.**
$3 \times (8 \div 8) =$ ☐

**f.**
$5 \times (32 \div 4) =$ ☐

**2.** Complete the missing parts.

**a.**
26,308

 thousands ☐ hundreds

**b.**
☐

 thousands ☐ hundreds

fourteen thousand one hundred sixty-nine

**c.**
80,716

 thousands  hundreds

## Preparing for Module 12

Complete these facts.

**a.**
$3 \times$ ☐ $= 12$

**b.**
☐ $\times 2 = 18$

**c.**
$4 \times$ ☐ $= 28$

**d.**
$4 \times$ ☐ $= 40$

**e.**
☐ $\times 9 = 27$

**f.**
☐ $\times 8 = 16$

**g.**
$7 \times$ ☐ $= 14$

**h.**
$8 \times 4 =$ ☐

**i.**
$5 \times$ ☐ $= 15$

**Step In**  **What are some reasons for rounding large numbers?**

How could you round the population of Lincoln County?

Welcome to Lincoln County

Population    46,214

Richard used a number line to help him round the population to the nearest **ten**.

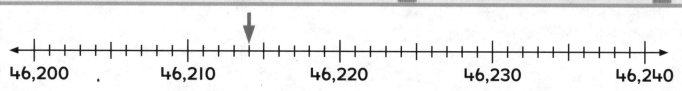

46,200        46,210        46,220        46,230        46,240

What is the population rounded to the nearest ten?

How does the halfway position between 46,210 and 46,220 on the number line help you round the number?

What happens if the number being rounded is halfway between two tens? How would you round 46,215 to the nearest ten?

**How could you use this number line to round the population of Lincoln County to the nearest hundred?**

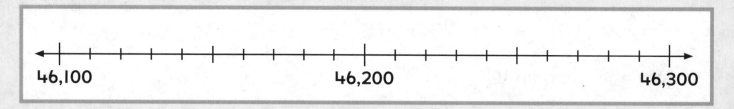

46,100                        46,200                        46,300

I look at the digits in the hundreds, tens, and ones places. 214 is closer to 200 than 300.

© ORIGO Education

1. Round each population to the nearest **ten**.
   Use the number line to help your thinking.

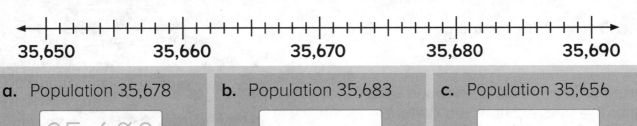

**a.** Population 35,678

35,680

**b.** Population 35,683

**c.** Population 35,656

2. Round each population to the nearest **hundred**.

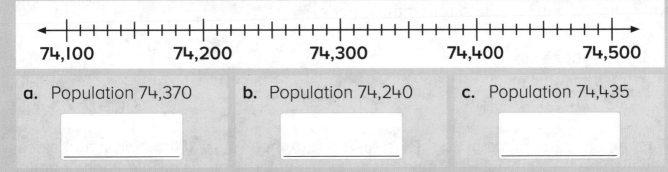

**a.** Population 74,370

**b.** Population 74,240

**c.** Population 74,435

3. Round each population to the nearest **hundred**.

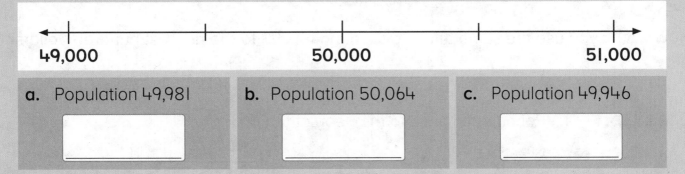

**a.** Population 49,981

**b.** Population 50,064

**c.** Population 49,946

**Step Ahead**

Imagine you round each number to the nearest ten thousand.
Write the letter **A** beside the numbers that will round to 20,000.

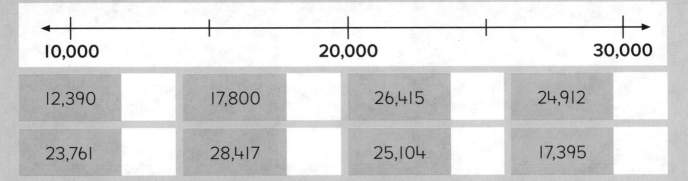

| 12,390 | | 17,800 | | 26,415 | | 24,912 | |
| 23,761 | | 28,417 | | 25,104 | | 17,395 | |

**Step In**

What is the price of this car?

$31,427

The retailer has decided to round this price to the nearest hundred dollars.

What is the new price of the car?
How do you know?

What digits did you look at to round the number?

Cary follows these steps.

| 3 1,④2 7 | 3 1,④2̲ 7 | 3 1,④2̲ 7 |
|---|---|---|
| First he finds the place to which he is rounding. | Then he looks at the next lowest place value. | If the digit in that place is greater than or equal to 5 then the number is rounded up. |

How would you use the same thinking to round 42,753 to the nearest hundred dollars?

**Step Up**

1. Round each price to the nearest **ten** dollars.

a.  $27,689

$_____

b.  $17,381

$_____

c.  $32,863

$_____

d.  $19,224

$_____

e.  $25,865

$_____

f.  $49,357

$_____

g.  $31,116

$_____

h.  $22,298

$_____

i.  $18,072

$_____

**2.** Round each price to the nearest **hundred** dollars.

**a.** $35,305

$_____

**b.** $21,290

$_____

**c.** $46,542

$_____

**d.** $36,455.

$_____

**e.** $28,185

$_____

**f.** $14,702

$_____

**g.** $31,116

$_____

**h.** $17,198

$_____

**i.** $57,049

$_____

**3.** Round each number to the nearest **ten** and **hundred**.

|  | 14,312 | 51,678 | 29,087 | 26,305 |
|---|---|---|---|---|
| Nearest Ten |  |  |  |  |
| Nearest Hundred |  |  |  |  |

## Step Ahead

Carmen rounds a number to the nearest ten. Her answer is 26,000.
She then rounds the same number to the nearest hundred. Her answer is 26,000.
She then rounds the same number to the nearest thousand. Her answer is 26,000.

Write five possible numbers Carmen could have rounded.

|  |  |  |  |  |
|---|---|---|---|---|

**Working Space**

## Computation Practice

★ For each of these, write the multiplication fact you would use to help figure out the division fact. Then write the quotients. Use the classroom clock to time yourself.

**Time Taken:**

**start**

$40 \div 8 = \boxed{\phantom{0}}$

$\boxed{\phantom{0}} \times \boxed{\phantom{0}} = \boxed{\phantom{0}}$

$28 \div 4 = \boxed{\phantom{0}}$

$\boxed{\phantom{0}} \times \boxed{\phantom{0}} = \boxed{\phantom{0}}$

$20 \div 5 = \boxed{\phantom{0}}$

$\boxed{\phantom{0}} \times \boxed{\phantom{0}} = \boxed{\phantom{0}}$

$16 \div 4 = \boxed{\phantom{0}}$

$\boxed{\phantom{0}} \times \boxed{\phantom{0}} = \boxed{\phantom{0}}$

$45 \div 5 = \boxed{\phantom{0}}$

$\boxed{\phantom{0}} \times \boxed{\phantom{0}} = \boxed{\phantom{0}}$

$12 \div 6 = \boxed{\phantom{0}}$

$\boxed{\phantom{0}} \times \boxed{\phantom{0}} = \boxed{\phantom{0}}$

$15 \div 3 = \boxed{\phantom{0}}$

$\boxed{\phantom{0}} \times \boxed{\phantom{0}} = \boxed{\phantom{0}}$

$16 \div 2 = \boxed{\phantom{0}}$

$\boxed{\phantom{0}} \times \boxed{\phantom{0}} = \boxed{\phantom{0}}$

$35 \div 5 = \boxed{\phantom{0}}$

$\boxed{\phantom{0}} \times \boxed{\phantom{0}} = \boxed{\phantom{0}}$

$18 \div 9 = \boxed{\phantom{0}}$

$\boxed{\phantom{0}} \times \boxed{\phantom{0}} = \boxed{\phantom{0}}$

$32 \div 8 = \boxed{\phantom{0}}$

$\boxed{\phantom{0}} \times \boxed{\phantom{0}} = \boxed{\phantom{0}}$

$25 \div 5 = \boxed{\phantom{0}}$

$\boxed{\phantom{0}} \times \boxed{\phantom{0}} = \boxed{\phantom{0}}$

$36 \div 4 = \boxed{\phantom{0}}$

$\boxed{\phantom{0}} \times \boxed{\phantom{0}} = \boxed{\phantom{0}}$

$10 \div 2 = \boxed{\phantom{0}}$

$\boxed{\phantom{0}} \times \boxed{\phantom{0}} = \boxed{\phantom{0}}$

**finish**

$30 \div 6 = \boxed{\phantom{0}}$

$\boxed{\phantom{0}} \times \boxed{\phantom{0}} = \boxed{\phantom{0}}$

$12 \div 4 = \boxed{\phantom{0}}$

$\boxed{\phantom{0}} \times \boxed{\phantom{0}} = \boxed{\phantom{0}}$

$14 \div 2 = \boxed{\phantom{0}}$

$\boxed{\phantom{0}} \times \boxed{\phantom{0}} = \boxed{\phantom{0}}$

## Ongoing Practice

**1.** Read the word problem. Then color the ⬭ beside the thinking you would use to figure out the answer.

**a.**
Jacinta saved $3 each week for 4 weeks.
Her mom also gave her $5.
How much money does she have?

- ⬭ (3 × 5) + 4
- ⬭ 3 × 4 + 5
- ⬭ 3 × (4 + 5)

**b.**
Mr. Rose had $20. He spent $8 then shared the change equally among his 3 grandchildren. How much money was in each share?

- ⬭ 20 − (8 ÷ 3)
- ⬭ 20 − 8 ÷ 3
- ⬭ (20 − 8) ÷ 3

**c.**
A six-pack of juice boxes costs $3.
If you bought 2 packs, how much change would you get from $10?

- ⬭ (6 × 2) − 10
- ⬭ 10 − (3 × 2)
- ⬭ 10 − (6 × 2)

**2.** Write each number in expanded form.

**a.**
46,123 _____

_____

**b.**
50,762 _____

_____

## Preparing for Module 12

Write the product for each part. Then write the total.

**a.**
5 × 10 = _____     5 × 5 = _____

5 × 15 = _____

**b.**
3 × 10 = _____     3 × 7 = _____

3 × 17 = _____

**Step In**   Do you think these two pieces of fruit will cost more or less than $1?

How would you calculate the total cost?

> 60¢ and 40¢ is 100¢.
> That's one dollar, and 5¢
> and 5¢ makes another 10¢.
> The total is $1 and 10¢.

Write an equation to show your thinking.

Calculate the total cost for each pair of prices.
Then write an equation to show your thinking.

| | | | | |
|---|---|---|---|---|
| ○ 85¢ | ○ 70¢ | $70 + 30 + 55 = 155$ | $_____ and | _____¢ |
| ○ 60¢ | ○ 55¢ | | $_____ and | _____¢ |
| ○ 75¢ | ○ 45¢ | | $_____ and | _____¢ |

**Step Up**   I.   Color coins that make a total of $1. Then write the total amount.

a.

$_____ and _____¢

b.

$_____ and _____¢

**2.** Calculate the total cost. Write an equation to show your thinking.

**a.**

| 95¢ | 45¢ |

Total $_____ and _____¢

**b.**

| 85¢ | 65¢ |

Total $_____ and _____¢

**c.**

| 95¢ | 75¢ |

Total $_____ and _____¢

**d.**

| 30¢ | 60¢ | 45¢ |

Total $_____ and _____¢

**e.**

| 75¢ | 40¢ | 30¢ |

Total $_____ and _____¢

---

**Step Ahead**

Ethan bought three pieces of fruit. The fruit cost $1 and 80¢ in total. He says that the apple was more than the banana and that the watermelon was the most expensive.

Write a possible price for each piece of fruit. Show your thinking.

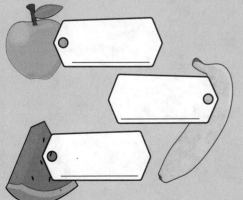

© ORIGO Education

**Step In**

Imagine you have these bills and coins. What bills and coins would you use to buy this magazine?

DOGS
$2 and 45¢

I would use 2 dollar bills and 2 quarters.
That's $2 and 50¢. I should get some change.

Can you pay the exact amount of money with no change given?

**Do you have enough money to buy this toy car?**

How much more money do you need to save?

$3 and 50¢

**Step Up**

1. Color the bills and coins that you would use to pay the exact price. No change will be given.

a. $6 and 37¢

b. $15 and 17¢

**2.** Draw simple pictures of bills and coins to show the **exact** price.

a.

○$7 and 42¢

b.

○ $3 and 8¢

c.

○$16 and 35¢

d.

○$3 and 89¢

**Step Ahead**    Draw bills and coins in the purse to help solve this problem.

Harvey has one $5 bill, 3 quarters, and a penny. He wants to buy a toy that costs $6 and 50¢. How much more money does he need to save?

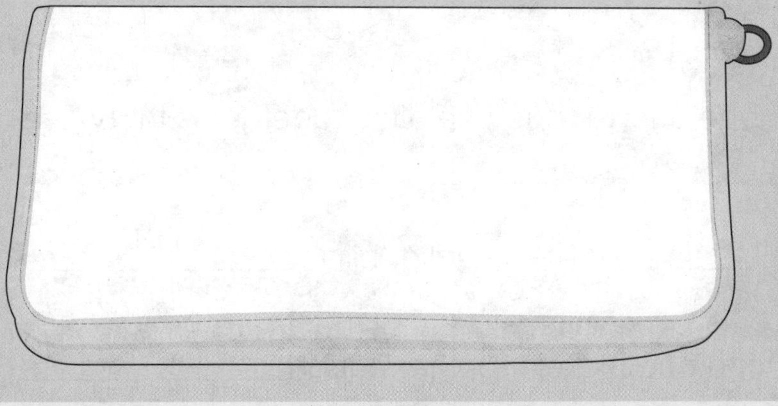

**Think and Solve**   Look at the equation.

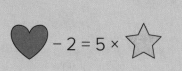

**a.** If ⭐ is 6, what is ❤? _____

**b.** If ⭐ is 7, what is ❤? _____

**c.** What are some other numbers for ⭐ and ❤ that make the equation true?

_____

_____

**Words at Work**  Choose and write words from the list to complete these sentences. Some words are not used.

**a.**
One dollar has the same value as four _____.

**b.**
Four nickels have the same value as _____ dimes.

**c.**
Three dollar bills, five quarters, _____ dimes, and three _____ together equal five _____.

**d.**
One quarter and one dime together is thirty-five _____.

**e.**
_____ dollar bills, _____ quarters, twelve dimes, and one nickel together equal _____ dollars.

nickels
dimes
two
quarters
dollars
four
five
cents
six
three

© ORIGO Education

| Month | Number of Movies |
|-------|------------------|
| June | 14 |
| July | 17 |
| August | 6 |
| September | 9 |

## Ongoing Practice

1. This table shows the number of movies watched by the Martinez family during the summer months. Complete the picture graph below to show the results.

☐ means 2 movies

### Movies Watched

| Month | | | | | | | | | | | |
|-------|--|--|--|--|--|--|--|--|--|--|--|
| June | | | | | | | | | | | |
| July | | | | | | | | | | | |
| August | | | | | | | | | | | |
| September | | | | | | | | | | | |

2. Write the number that was expanded.

a. _____

$(7 \times 10,000) + (8 \times 1,000) + (2 \times 100) + (5 \times 10) + (8 \times 1)$

b. _____

$(5 \times 10,000) + (1 \times 1,000) + (8 \times 100) + (3 \times 10) + (7 \times 1)$

c. _____

$(3 \times 10,000) + (4 \times 1,000) + (1 \times 100) + (7 \times 10) + (6 \times 1)$

## Preparing for Module 12     Circle the pyramids.

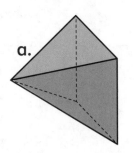
a.

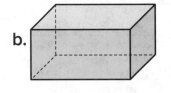
b.

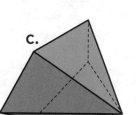
c.

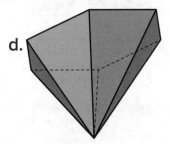
d.

# 11.9 Money: Calculating change (cents)

**Step In**

Bianca has **2 quarters** in her wallet. Does she have enough money to buy this stamp?

How much change should she get?

**Callum has a dollar bill, 2 quarters, and 1 dime in his wallet.**

Does he have enough money to buy this folder?
What bills and coins could he use?

$1 and 40¢

Callum pays for the folder and puts the change in his wallet.
How much money does he have left to spend?

**Step Up**

1. Draw the coins you would receive as change.

| | Price | Amount you pay | Change you receive |
|---|---|---|---|
| **a.** | 30¢ | QUARTER DOLLAR, ONE DIME | |
| **b.** | 40¢ | QUARTER DOLLAR, QUARTER DOLLAR | |
| **c.** | 65¢ | ONE DOLLAR | |
| **d.** | 55¢ | QUARTER DOLLAR, QUARTER DOLLAR, QUARTER DOLLAR | |

**2.** Color the bills and coins that you would use to pay the price.
Then write the change that you should receive.

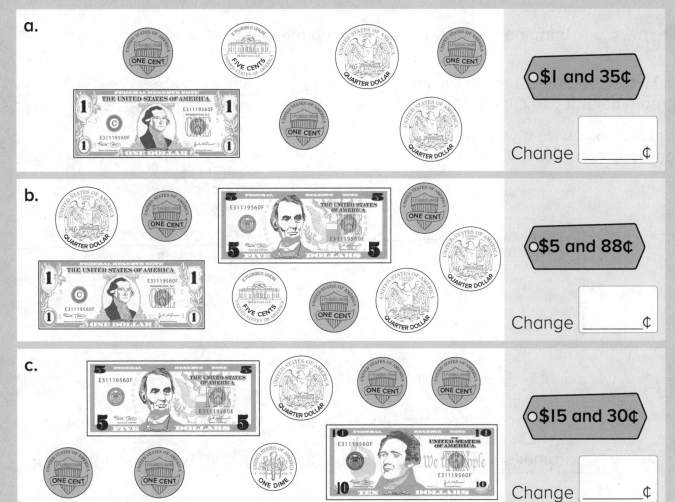

a.
$1 and 35¢

Change _____ ¢

b.
$5 and 88¢

Change _____ ¢

c.
$15 and 30¢

Change _____ ¢

---

**Step Ahead**

Solve this problem. Show your thinking by drawing pictures or writing equations.

Evan has $2 and 45¢ in his wallet.
He has some bills and some coins.
He buys a soda and has 18¢ left over.

How much did he pay for the soda?

**Step In** Imagine you only had a half-cup measure.

How would you measure out all the ingredients that use cups in this recipe?

What would you do if you only had a **one-cup** measure?

**Lemon and Pecan Muffins**

5 cups of flour
2 cups of sugar
2 and a half cups of milk
2 eggs
2 sticks of butter
I cup of lemon juice
Half cup of chopped pecans

**Step Up**

I. Your teacher will give you some containers to measure.
Estimate the capacity of each container first.
Then use the measuring containers to find the exact capacity.

| a. | Container | My estimate (cups) | Actual capacity (cups) |
|---|---|---|---|
| | A | | |
| | B | | |
| | C | | |
| | D | | |

| b. | Container | My estimate (pints) | Actual capacity (pints) |
|---|---|---|---|
| | A | | |
| | B | | |
| | C | | |
| | D | | |

Estimate the capacity of each container first.
Then use the measuring containers to find the exact capacity.

| c. Container | My estimate (quarts) | Actual capacity (quarts) |
|---|---|---|
| A | | |
| B | | |
| C | | |
| D | | |

2. a. How many cups does Container C hold? ☐

   b. How many pints does Container C hold? ☐

   c. How many quarts does Container C hold? ☐

   d. What do you notice about the number of cups, pints, and quarts for Container C?

   _____
   _____
   _____
   _____

**Step Ahead**   Write numbers to complete this table.

| Quarts | 1 | 2 | 3 | 6 | | | 33 |
|---|---|---|---|---|---|---|---|
| Pints | 2 | 4 | | | 16 | 48 | |

**Computation Practice**

**Why did fifteen people walk out of the restaurant at nine o'clock?**

⭐ Complete the equations. Write each letter above its matching answer in the grid below. Some letters appear more than once.

170 + 29 = ____ **y**

252 – 47 = ____ **f**

333 – 79 = ____ **g**

380 – 27 = ____ **s**

38 + 361 = ____ **l**

135 + 37 = ____ **e**

56 + 124 = ____ **d**

207 + 48 = ____ **n**

453 – 427 = ____ **h**

268 – 239 = ____ **r**

140 – 65 = ____ **t**

65 + 129 = ____ **i**

243 + 49 = ____ **m**

71 + 309 = ____ **a**

75    26    172    199         26    380    180         380    399    399

205    194    255    194    353    26    172    180

172    380    75    194    255    254         75    26    172    194    29

292    172    380    399    353

## Ongoing Practice

| Activity | Number of votes |
|---|---|
| Television | 10 |
| Homework | 5 |
| Reading | 19 |
| Sports | 16 |

**1.** This table shows the favorite after-school activities of Grade 3 students. Complete the bar graph below to show the results.

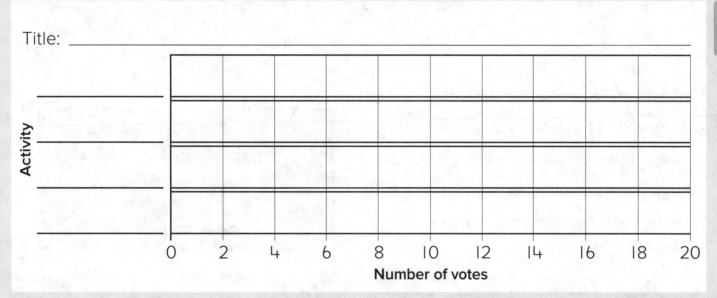

Title: _____

Activity

Number of votes

0  2  4  6  8  10  12  14  16  18  20

FROM 3.6.10

**2.** Write these numbers in order from **least** to **greatest**.

FROM 3.11.4

19,418     14,819     19,481     14,891     14,198     19,184

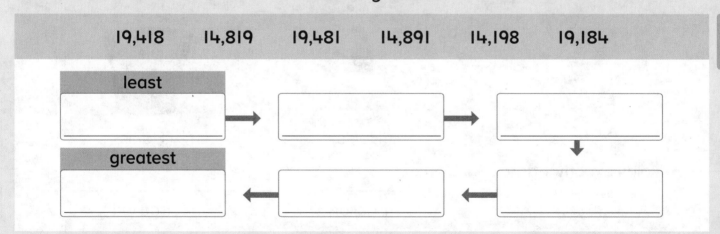

least

greatest

## Preparing for Module 12    Complete this chart.

| Object | Vertices | Straight edges | Curved edges | Flat faces | Curved surfaces |
|---|---|---|---|---|---|
| a. | | | | | |
| b. | | | | | |

© ORIGO Education

**Step In**   What do you know about cups, pints, and quarts?

Cups, pints, and quarts are units of liquid volume or capacity. They can be used to measure how much a container can hold.

**What do you know about gallons?**

One gallon **is equivalent to** four quarts.

One quart **is equivalent to** two pints.

One pint **is equivalent to** two cups.

How can you calculate the number of cups in one gallon?

There is a short way to write these units of liquid volume or capacity.

- gallon can be written as gal
- quart can be written as qt
- pint can be written as pt

**Step Up**   I.  Write **less than**, **about**, or **more than** to describe how much you think each container holds when compared to one gallon.

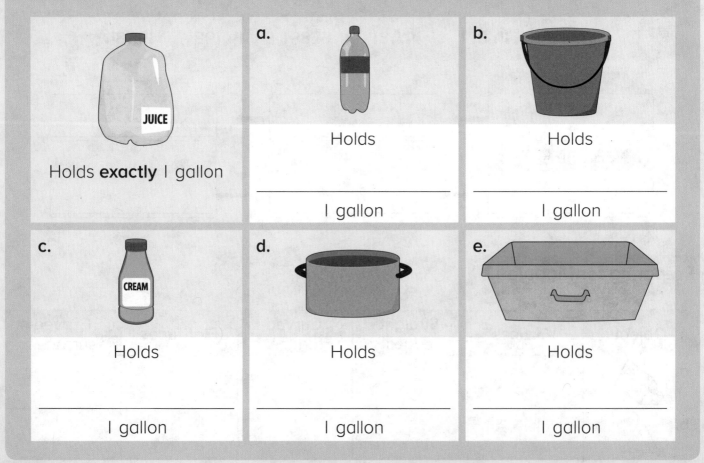

Holds **exactly** I gallon

a.

Holds

_____

I gallon

b.

Holds

_____

I gallon

c.

Holds

_____

I gallon

d.

Holds

_____

I gallon

e.

Holds

_____

I gallon

**2.** Write **less than**, **about**, or **more than** to describe the amount of water that each container holds.

**a.**

Holds
_____
1 gallon

**b.**

Holds
_____
1 gallon

**c.**
Holds
_____
1 gallon

**d.**
Holds
_____
1 gallon

**3.** Each container holds one gallon. Write the number of pints or quarts that you would add to fill the container.

**a.**

_____ more pints make 1 gallon.

**b.**
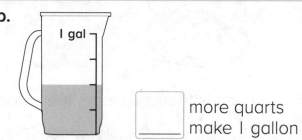
_____ more quarts make 1 gallon

| **Step Ahead** | Use the information on page 426 to help solve this problem. |

Lifen's container holds 2 quarts, Henry's container holds 7 cups, and Anya's container holds 5 pints. Whose container holds the most?

_____

Show your thinking below.

**Step In**  How could you figure out which container holds the most?

What attribute are you trying to measure?

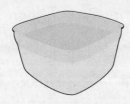

**How could you figure out which grocery bag is the heaviest to carry?**
What attribute are you now trying to measure?

What are some situations where the length of an object is important to know?

**Step Up**

1. Read each problem. Then color the card that shows the measurement attribute that you would investigate to solve each problem.

a. Anna wants to pour some leftover soup into a container. She wants to know what container size to choose.

| capacity | mass | length |

b. The maximum carry load for an elevator is 800 kg. 12 people want to enter the elevator. Will the elevator carry the load?

| capacity | mass | length |

c. 200 gallons of water are pumped into a swimming pool each minute. How long will it take to fill the swimming pool with water?

| capacity | mass | length |

d. Hernando wants to fence his property. How can he figure out the number of fencing panels he needs to buy?

| capacity | mass | length |

**2.** Solve each problem. Show your thinking.

**a.** Chloe needs 6 cups of flour, and 2 cups of coconut. She only has a half-cup measure. How many half-cups of flour does she need to pour into the bowl?

_____ half-cups

**b.** A store manager notices that 3 boxes of ice cream can no longer be sold. Each box holds 24 pints of ice cream. How many pints of ice cream must be thrown out?

_____ pt

**c.** Marvin pours water from a 1-gallon bottle into some smaller bottles. He finds that each gallon bottle fills about 6 small bottles. He has 20 small bottles to fill. How many 1-gallon bottles should he buy?

_____ bottles

**d.** Peter is making 4 bowls of fruit punch for a party. He needs 2 qt of lemonade, 1 qt of apple juice, and $\frac{1}{2}$ qt of orange juice to make one bowl. How many quarts of orange juice should he buy?

_____ qt

---

**Step Ahead**  Use the relationship between cups, pints, quarts, and gallons to solve this problem.

Leftover juice is poured into a 1-gallon container. Afterward, the 1-gallon container is $\frac{3}{4}$ full.

How many cups of fruit juice were poured into the 1-gallon container?

_____ cups

## Think and Solve

Read the clues. Write the matching letter beside each type of muffin.

 **Clues**

- Twice as many pecan as apple muffins were sold.
- 15 apple muffins were sold.
- 27 more chocolate than berry muffins were sold.

**Muffins Sold**    means 6 muffins

| | | | | | | | | |
|---|---|---|---|---|---|---|---|---|
| **A** | | | | | | | | |
| **B** | | | | | | | | |
| **C** | | | | | | | | |
| **D** | | | | | | | | |

Pecan _____    Apple _____    Berry _____    Chocolate _____

## Words at Work

Write the answer for each clue in the grid. Use words from the list. Some words are not used.

**Clues Across**

2. Two pints is the same amount as four ___.
5. There are sixteen pints in two ___.
7. Thirty-one cups is ___ two gallons.

**Clues Down**

1. Four cups is the same amount as one ___.
3. One ___ is more than one cup.
4. The short way to write a gallon is ___.
6. One pint is ___ than one gallon.

pint
about
less
more
gallons
cups
quart
gal

© ORIGO Education

***ORIGO Stepping Stones*** · Grade 3 · 11.12

**Ongoing Practice**

1. These line plots show the distances run each day by an athlete during training.

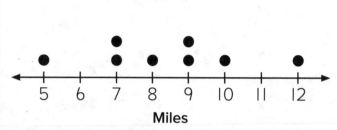

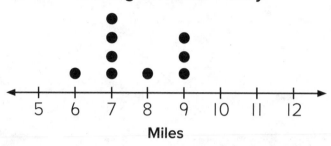

a. In which month did the athlete train for the greater number of days?

b. In which month was the longest run?

c. What is the difference between the total distances run in April and May?

_____ miles

2. Round each population to the nearest **hundred**. Use the number line to help your thinking.

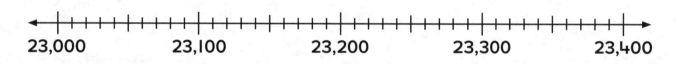

a. Population 23,156

b. Population 23,308

c. Population 23,279

**Preparing for Module 12**

Draw a rectangle on the grid to match each description. Then use multiplication to calculate the area.

a.

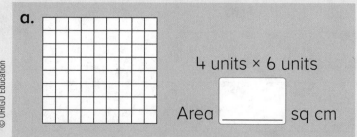

4 units × 6 units

Area _____ sq cm

b.

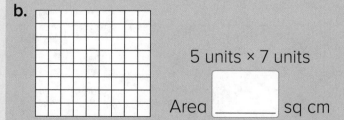

5 units × 7 units

Area _____ sq cm

**Step In**  Four friends share the cost of this gift.

Do they have to pay more or less than $10 each?
How do you know?

How could you figure out the amount that they each have to pay?

Eva draws this picture.

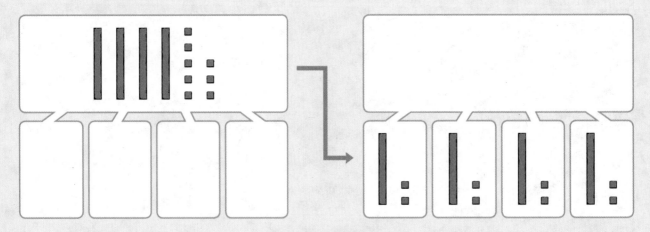

How does she figure out the amount that each person should pay?

> She shows the total cost with blocks.
> Then she shares the blocks among the 4 friends.

**Step Up**  1. Draw blocks in the smaller parts to show each share.
Then complete the equation.

$69 \div 3 = \boxed{\phantom{00}}$

**2.** Draw blocks in the large part to show the number being shared. Then draw blocks in the small parts to show the number in each share. Complete the equation.

**a.**
$48 \div 2 =$ ☐

**b.**
$39 \div 3 =$ ☐

**c.**
$84 \div 4 =$ ☐

**d.**
$86 \div 2 =$ ☐

**e.**
$93 \div 3 =$ ☐

**f.**
$44 \div 4 =$ ☐

**Step Ahead**

A group of friends shared the cost of a gift. Each person paid $23. How many friends might there have been in the group? What was the total cost?

There were  friends.    The total cost was  $_____ .

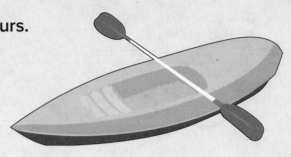

**Step In**   It costs **$42** to rent a canoe for 3 hours.

How much do you think it will cost to rent a canoe for one hour?

Do you think it will cost more or less than $20? How did you decide?

Brady draws this picture to figure it out.

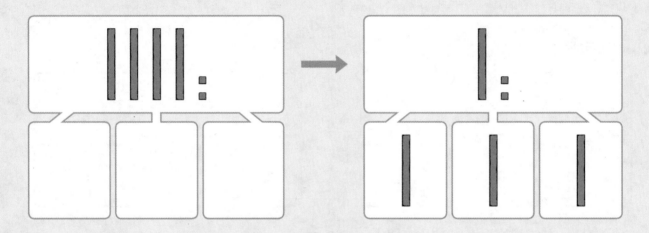

How can he share the leftover blocks?

He can regroup the blocks. I tens block can be exchanged for 10 ones blocks. That makes 12 ones. It's easy to share 12 ones among 3.

How much does it cost to rent a canoe for one hour?

**Step Up**   I.   Draw a different quantity of tens and ones blocks that can then be used to calculate 56 shared among 4.

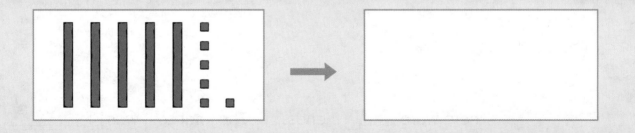

**2.** In each picture, I tens block has been regrouped for 10 ones blocks.
Draw blocks in the small parts to show each share. Then complete the equation.

**a.**
$52 \div 4 =$ ☐

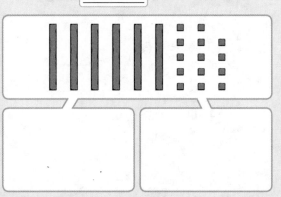

**b.**
$48 \div 3 =$ ☐

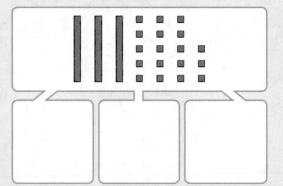

**c.**
$74 \div 2 =$ ☐

**d.**
$92 \div 4 =$ ☐

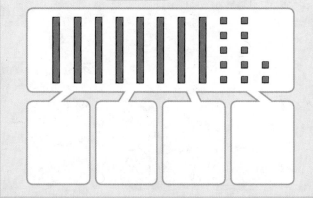

**3.** Complete each equation. You can use blocks or draw pictures on page 470.

**a.**
$65 \div 5 =$ ☐

**b.**
$56 \div 2 =$ ☐

**c.**
$84 \div 6 =$ ☐

**d.**
$51 \div 3 =$ ☐

**Step Ahead**

Four friends plan to share the cost of a gift. They will each pay $21. Then three more of their friends decide to share the cost of the gift. How much will each friend pay now?
Show your thinking.

$ _____

## Computation Practice

★ Complete the equations. Then write each letter above its matching product at the bottom of the page to reveal a fact about the natural world. Some letters appear more than once.

7 × 7 = ___ **a**     3 × 6 = ___ **s**     8 × 6 = ___ **u**

8 × 8 = ___ **n**     4 × 4 = ___ **r**     5 × 4 = ___ **w**

7 × 3 = ___ **e**     7 × 6 = ___ **t**     9 × 8 = ___ **l**

4 × 6 = ___ **d**     8 × 1 = ___ **c**     0 × 7 = ___ **b**

2 × 7 = ___ **o**     9 × 9 = ___ **g**     6 × 6 = ___ **m**

9 × 3 = ___ **k**

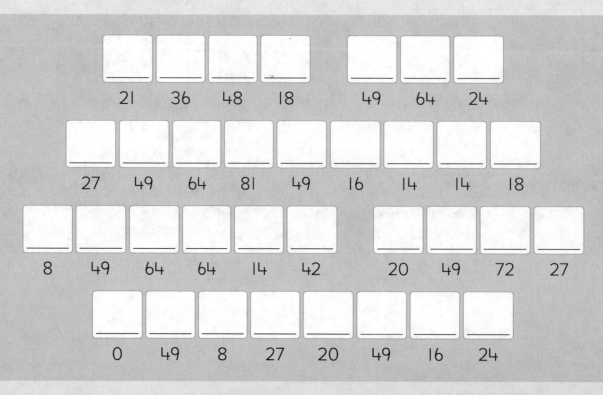

☐ ☐ ☐ ☐   ☐ ☐ ☐
21 36 48 18   49 64 24

☐ ☐ ☐ ☐ ☐ ☐ ☐ ☐ ☐
27 49 64 81 49 16 14 14 18

☐ ☐ ☐ ☐ ☐ ☐   ☐ ☐ ☐ ☐
8 49 64 64 14 42   20 49 72 27

☐ ☐ ☐ ☐ ☐ ☐ ☐
0 49 8 27 20 49 16 24

**1.** Draw bills and coins to match the amount below.

| $ | ¢ |
|---|---|

three dollars and forty-five cents

**2.** Draw blocks in the large part to show the number being shared.
Then draw blocks in the small parts to show the number in each share.
Complete the equation.

**a.**

$48 \div 4 =$ [ ]

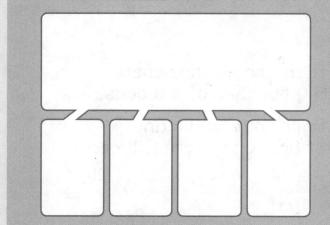

**b.**

$69 \div 3 =$ [ ]

**Preparing for Next Year**   Draw beads on each abacus to represent the number.

**a.**

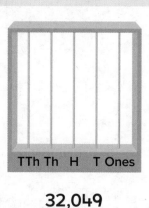

TTh Th  H   T Ones

32,049

**b.**

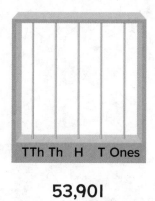

TTh Th  H   T Ones

53,901

**c.**

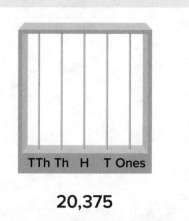

TTh Th  H   T Ones

20,375

# Division: Thinking multiplication to divide two-digit numbers

**Step In**

Lulu is decorating the gym for the dance.
She decides to put 3 balloons in each bunch.
There are 45 balloons in total.

How many bunches of balloons can she make?

Kyle starts by drawing pictures and using skip counting to help him figure it out.

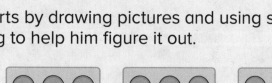

| 3 | 6 | 9 | 12 | 15 |

What other numbers will he say?

How does the picture help him figure out the number of bunches?

Carol tries using what she knows about decomposing numbers and multiplication.

If 3 × 10 is 30, then I know that there will be at least 10 bunches of balloons.

Now I need to figure out how many more bunches of balloons there will be.

**Step Up**

I. Skip count by 4 to complete the equation.
Draw simple pictures to show your thinking.

$52 \div 4 =$ _____

**2.** Complete each equation. Show your thinking.

**a.**

$36 \div 3 = \boxed{\phantom{00}}$

**b.**

$75 \div 5 = \boxed{\phantom{00}}$

**c.**

$60 \div 4 = \boxed{\phantom{00}}$

**d.**

$51 \div 3 = \boxed{\phantom{00}}$

**Step Ahead**   Solve the problem. Show your thinking.

Third grade is going on a camping trip. The teacher says that 5 students fit in each tent. 67 students are going. 10 students are unable to attend. How many tents will be needed for the students?

$\boxed{\phantom{0000}}$ tents

**Step In**     4 friends share the cost of this meal.

 **TONI'S PIZZA PARLOR**

4 meals plus drinks

Total $68

How could you estimate the amount of money
that each person should pay?

Do you think the amount will be more or less than $10? ... $20?
How did you form your estimate?

4 × 10 = 40. $10 each is not enough.
4 × 20 = 80. $20 each is too much.

So, the amount must be between $10 and $20.

**It costs $72 for a group of 3 friends to eat at a different restaurant.
They decide to split the cost.**

About how much should they each pay?

Do you think the amount will be more or less than $20? How do you know?

**Step Up**     1.  Read the division problem. Then complete each multiplication
equation to help you form an estimate.

| a.  54 ÷ 3 | b.  78 ÷ 6 | c.  80 ÷ 5 |
|---|---|---|
| 3 × 10 = ____ | 6 × 10 = ____ | 5 × 10 = ____ |
| 3 × 20 = ____ | 6 × 20 = ____ | 5 × 20 = ____ |
| Estimate | Estimate | Estimate |

© ORIGO Education

**2.** Read the problem. Then write your estimate. Show your thinking.

**a.** 3 friends share the cost of a taxi. The fare is $57. About how much should each person pay?

$_____

**b.** Jose has 72 yards of wire. He cuts the wire into 4 pieces about the same length. About how long is each piece?

_____ yards

**c.** A farmer collects 70 eggs. The eggs are put into cartons. Each carton holds 6 eggs. About how many cartons are needed?

_____ cartons

**d.** Terek spent about 45 minutes on the phone. He made 3 calls. Each call was about the same length. About how long was each call?

_____ minutes

**3.** Estimate each quotient. Circle the card if the quotient is greater than 20.

| 63 ÷ 3 | 96 ÷ 6 | 64 ÷ 4 | 92 ÷ 4 | 87 ÷ 3 |

**Step Ahead**

Circle the chairs you think are the better buy. Then write how you formed your decision.

_____

_____

_____

_____

**Store A**
3 chairs for $60

**Store B**
5 chairs for $80

**Think and Solve**  The numbers in the circles are the sums of the rows and columns. Write the missing numbers inside each shape. Then complete the equations.

For example,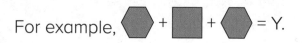

X = _____    Y = _____

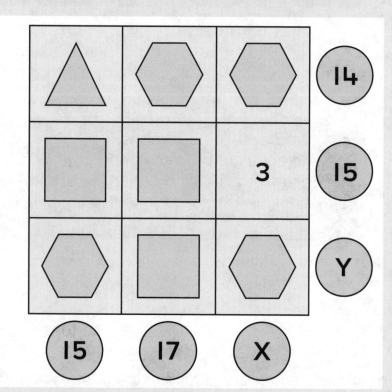

**Words at Work** Imagine your friend was away from school when you learned about dividing two-digit numbers. Write how you could use the think-multiplication strategy to calculate 72 ÷ 6.

## Ongoing Practice

**1.** Color the bills and coins that you would use to pay the price. Then write the change that you should receive.

**a.**

 $1 and 72¢

Change _____

**b.**

$6 and 90¢

Change _____

**2.** Complete each equation. Show your thinking.

**a.**

$84 \div 4 =$ _____

**b.**

$85 \div 5 =$ _____

## Preparing for Next Year

Write each number in expanded form.

**a.** 72,095 _____

**b.** 21,408 _____

**c.** 50,954 _____

**Step In**

92 laptops have been donated to a school district. The laptops are shared equally among 4 schools.

How could you estimate the number of laptops that each school should receive?

Do you think the number will be more or less than 10? ...20? How did you decide?

4 × **10** = 40. 10 laptops is too few.
4 × **20** = 80. 20 laptops is close.
4 × **30** = 120. 30 laptops is too many.

Britney knows that if 80 laptops were donated, then each school would receive 20 laptops.

More than 80 laptops were donated, so she decides to count by 4s from 80. She stops at 92.

How does this help her figure out the answer?

How many laptops are donated to each school?

**Step Up**

1. Read the division problem. Then complete each multiplication equation to help you form an estimate.

**a.** 81 ÷ 3

3 × **10** = _____

3 × **20** = _____

3 × **30** = _____

Estimate

_____

**b.** 52 ÷ 4

4 × **10** = _____

4 × **20** = _____

4 × **30** = _____

Estimate

_____

**c.** 99 ÷ 3

3 × **10** = _____

3 × **20** = _____

3 × **30** = _____

Estimate

_____

**2.** Complete each equation. Show your thinking.

**a.**

$63 ÷ 3 = \boxed{\phantom{00}}$

**b.**

$90 ÷ 5 = \boxed{\phantom{00}}$

**c.**

$96 ÷ 4 = \boxed{\phantom{00}}$

**3.** Solve each problem. Show your thinking.

**a.** 75 tickets are sold over 5 days. The same number of tickets are sold each day. How many tickets are sold on the third day?

$\boxed{\phantom{00}}$ tickets

**b.** 78 craft sticks are put on a tray. Each student takes 3 craft sticks. There are none left. How many students are in the class?

$\boxed{\phantom{00}}$ students

**Step Ahead**  Write a word problem to match this equation.  $68 ÷ 4 = 17$

_____

_____

_____

| Step In | Look at the amount of opening between the two shaded sides of the shape on the left below. |

Compare it to the amount of opening between the two shaded sides of the **shape on the right** below.

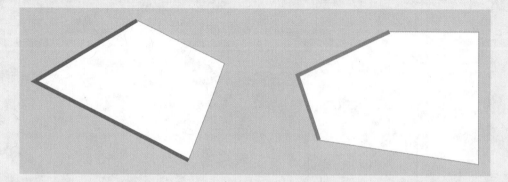

Which pair of sides has the greater amount of opening between them? How could you check?

| Step Up | 1. Color the corners green that match a green pattern block corner. Color the corners orange that match an orange pattern block corner. Color the corners yellow that match a yellow pattern block corner. |

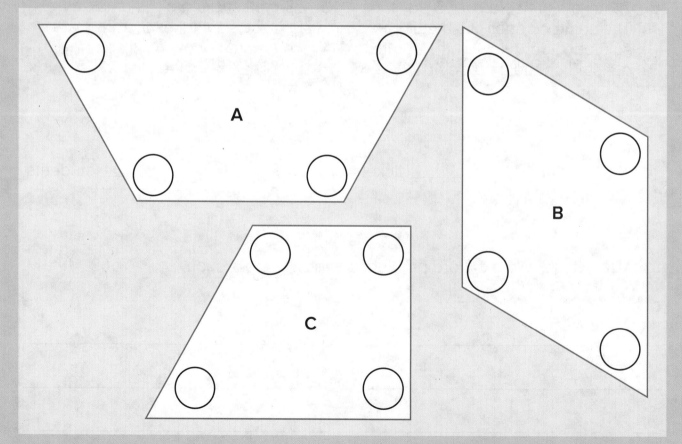

**2.** Color the corners green that match a green pattern block corner.
Color the corners orange that match an orange pattern block corner.
Color the corners yellow that match a yellow pattern block corner.

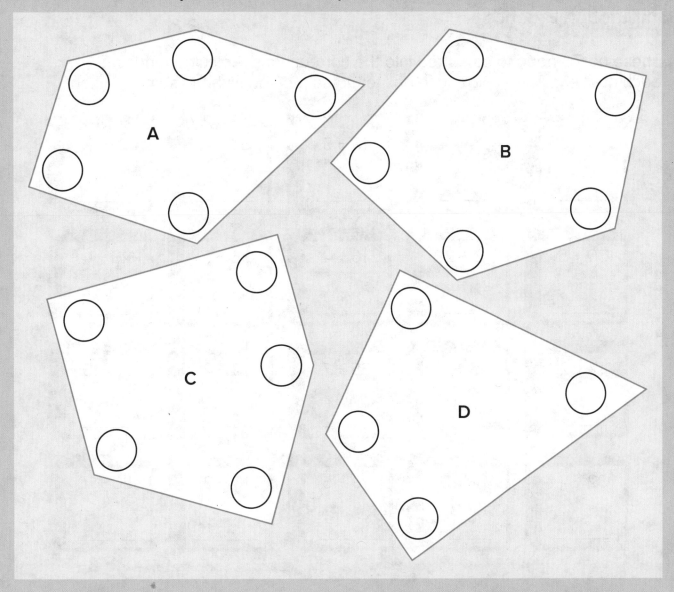

**Step Ahead**

Draw a hexagon with one corner that fits an orange pattern block corner.

## Computation Practice

★ These boxes need to be sorted into the correct vans. Calculate and write each quotient. Then color each box to match the van with the same quotient.

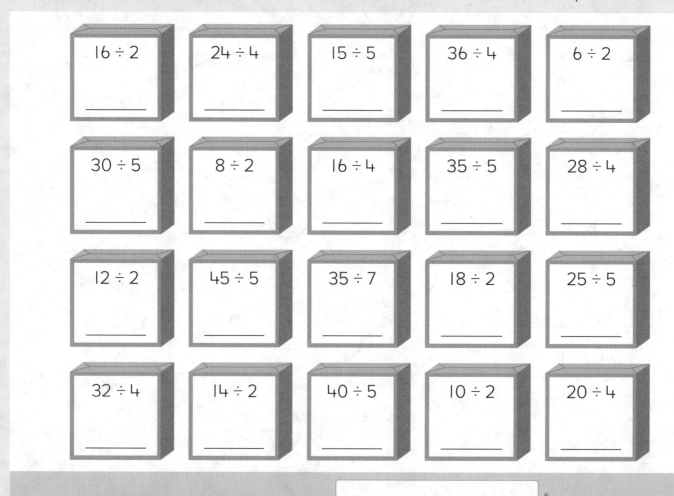

| 16 ÷ 2 | 24 ÷ 4 | 15 ÷ 5 | 36 ÷ 4 | 6 ÷ 2 |
| 30 ÷ 5 | 8 ÷ 2 | 16 ÷ 4 | 35 ÷ 5 | 28 ÷ 4 |
| 12 ÷ 2 | 45 ÷ 5 | 35 ÷ 7 | 18 ÷ 2 | 25 ÷ 5 |
| 32 ÷ 4 | 14 ÷ 2 | 40 ÷ 5 | 10 ÷ 2 | 20 ÷ 4 |

Which city will receive the most boxes? _____

DETROIT 7   DENVER 9   LAS VEGAS 6

SEATTLE 3   ATLANTA 8   PORTLAND 5   EL PASO 4

© ORIGO Education

1. Write meters or centimeters to show the unit you would use to measure these objects.

a. width of a student desk _____

b. length of the classroom _____

c. height of a door _____

d. length of your shoe _____

FROM 2.9.9 and 2.9.11

2. Read the problem. Then write your estimate. Show your thinking.

a. 4 friends share the cost of a taxi. The fare is $57. About how much should each person pay?

$_____

b. Emma uses 62 yards of fabric. She makes 4 stage curtains the same length. About how long is each curtain?

_____ yards

FROM 3.12.4

**Preparing for Next Year**  a. Write the numbers that are 10 less and 10 greater.

| 10 less | | | | | | |
|---|---|---|---|---|---|---|
| | 2,905 | 967 | 1,511 | 7,998 | 496 | 643 |
| 10 greater | | | | | | |

b. Write the numbers that are 100 less and 100 greater.

| 100 less | | | | | | |
|---|---|---|---|---|---|---|
| | 2,905 | 967 | 1,511 | 7,998 | 496 | 643 |
| 100 greater | | | | | | |

**Step In**  Follow these steps to make a tool to help measure angles.

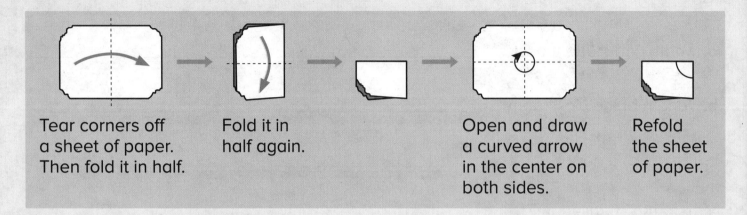

Tear corners off a sheet of paper. Then fold it in half.

Fold it in half again.

Open and draw a curved arrow in the center on both sides.

Refold the sheet of paper.

When the paper is opened out, you can place a strip on it and make the strip turn to line up along the creases.

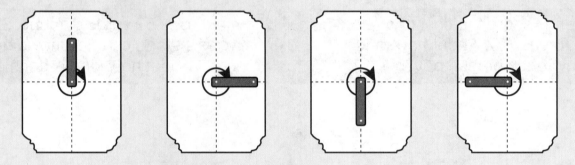

What fraction of a full turn is the strip moving each time?

After the strip turns four times it has made one full turn around a point. This is shown by the circle in the middle.

What fraction of the circle can you see when the paper is folded again?

This tool is called a quarter-turn tester.

What fraction of a full turn can it measure when it is folded?

**Step Up**  Use the quarter-turn tester to help you measure each corner of the shapes on page 453.

a. Color the corners red which the tester fits exactly.

b. Color the corners blue which are larger than the corner of the tester.

c. Color the corners green which are smaller than the corner of the tester.

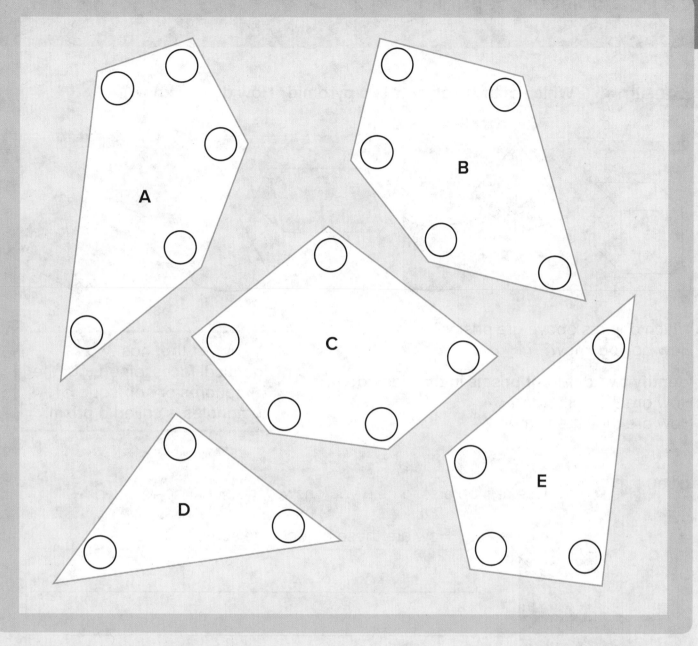

**Step Ahead**

Fold your quarter-turn tester like this. This tester can now measure one-eighth of a full turn.

**a.** Measure the corners of the shapes above using the eighth-turn tester. Circle the corners which the new tester fits exactly.

**b.** Draw a hexagon that has an eighth-turn corner.

**Step In**

Which of these objects is a pyramid? How do you know?

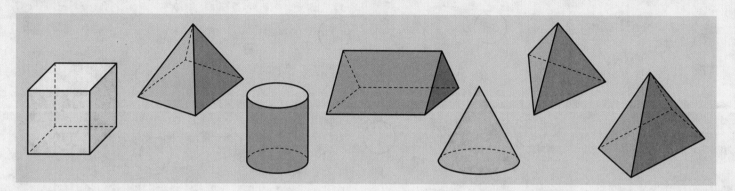

Which objects above are prisms?
How do you know?

**Identify two different prisms in the classroom.**
How are they different?
How are they the same?

> ℹ An object that has two identical faces joined together by squares or non-square rectangles is called a **prism**.

**Step Up**

1. Look at this pair of objects.
   Use real objects to help you answer the questions.

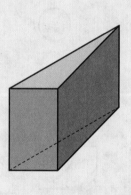

   **a.** How are these objects the same?

   _____

   _____

   _____

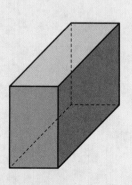

   **b.** How are these objects different?

   _____

   _____

   _____

**2.** Compare these two objects.

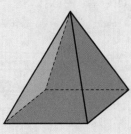

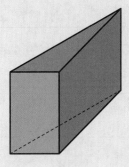

**a.** How are these objects the same?

**b.** How are these objects different?

**Step Ahead**  Circle the objects that are prisms.

a.
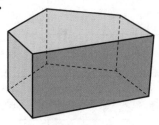

b.
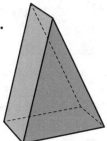

c.
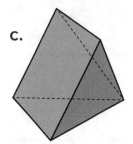

d.
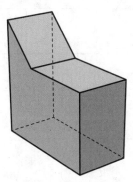

e.
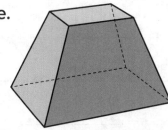

f.
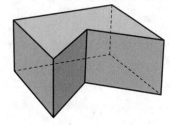

g.
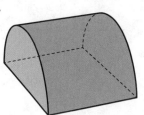

**Think and Solve**

This bag is full of marbles. There are at least 2 of each type of marble.

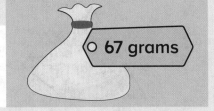

Some of the marbles weigh 1 gram.
Some of the marbles weigh 5 grams.
Some of the marbles weigh 25 grams.

**a.** How many 5-gram marbles are in the bag? _____

**b.** Show your thinking.

**Words at Work**   Explain what a quarter-turn tester is and how it is used to measure.

## Ongoing Practice

FROM 3.11.11

1. Write **less than**, **about**, or **more than** to describe the amount of water that each container holds.

**a.**

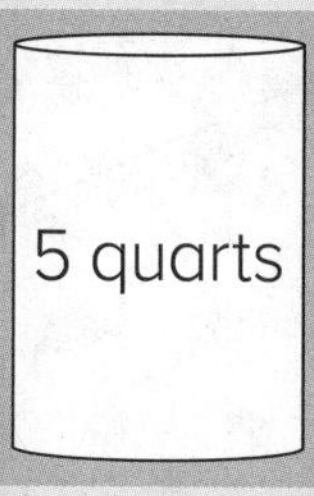

5 quarts

Holds ____________ 1 gallon

**b.**

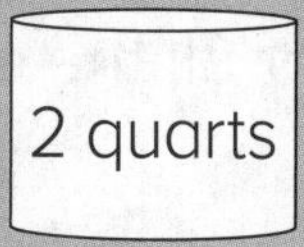

2 quarts

Holds ____________ 1 gallon

**c.**

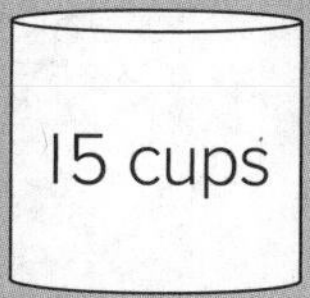

15 cups

Holds ____________ 1 gallon

**d.**

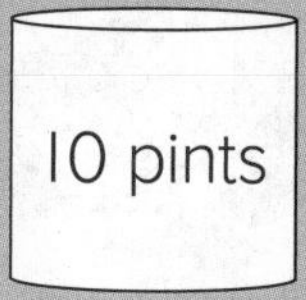

10 pints

Holds ____________ 1 gallon

FROM 3.12.5

2. Complete each equation. Show your thinking.

**a.** $96 \div 8 =$ ☐

**b.** $80 \div 5 =$ ☐

## Preparing for Next Year

Complete the equations. You can draw blocks to help your thinking.

**a.** Double 32 is ☐

**b.** Double 45 is ☐

**Step In**   What do you know about this object?

How many vertices are there?

Use a color pencil to trace over all the edges.
How many edges are there?

How many faces does the prism have?
What is the prism called? How do you know?

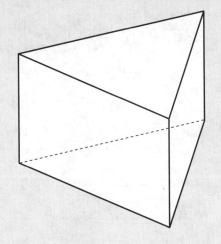

Look at each object below. How many vertices, edges, and faces does each have?

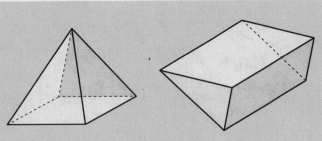

When two surfaces meet, they make an **edge**.

When three or more edges meet, they make a **vertex**. When there is more than one vertex, they are called **vertices**.

**Step Up**   1. a.   Use real objects to help you complete this table.
The base of each object is shaded.

| Prisms | | | |
|---|---|---|---|
| Number of faces | | | |
| Number of vertices | | | |
| Shape of base | | | |
| Number of sides on base | | | |

**b.** Look at the information in the table on page 458.
Write about the patterns you notice.

---

**2. a.** Complete this table.

| Pyramids | 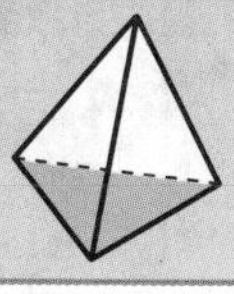 | 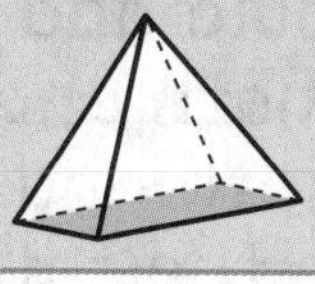 | 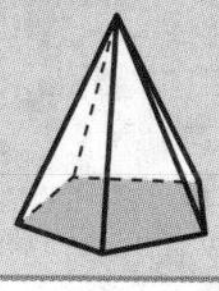 |
|---|---|---|---|
| Number of faces | | | |
| Number of vertices | | | |
| Shape of base | | | |
| Number of sides on base | | | |

**b.** Write about the patterns you notice.

---

**Step Ahead**

Think about a pyramid that has a hexagon as its base. How many faces, vertices, and edges does it have? Write how you figured it out.

Faces

Vertices

Edges

**Step In**

Jack is building a fence to make a chicken coop. This is his plan.

What is the total length of the fence?
How could you figure it out?

I could add the side lengths, or I could add the length and the width and double the total.

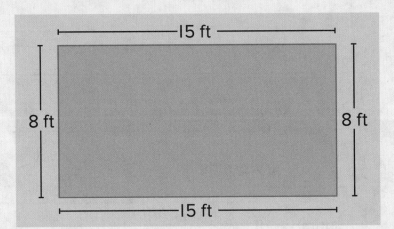

Perimeter is another name for the total distance around a shape.

How could you figure out the perimeter of this square?

Complete this equation to show how to calculate the perimeter.

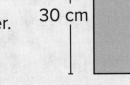

30 cm

☐ + ☐ + ☐ + ☐ = ☐

**Step Up**

1. Use the centimeter rulers to figure out the perimeter of this rectangle. Show your thinking.

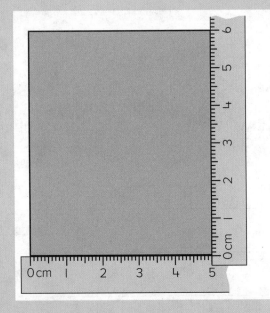

Perimeter _____ cm

**2.** This is a picture of a large field. Calculate the perimeter. Show your thinking.

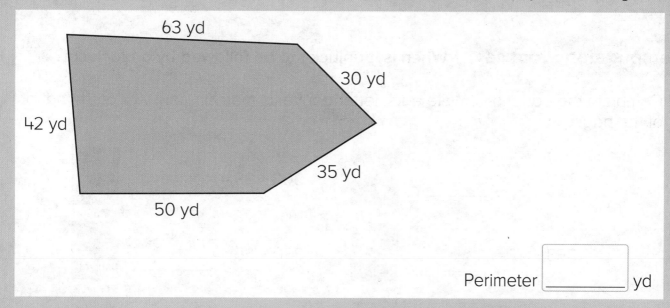

63 yd

30 yd

42 yd

35 yd

50 yd

Perimeter _____ yd

**3.** Look at the perimeter. Then calculate the length of the unknown side.
Show your thinking.

**Perimeter = 275 m**

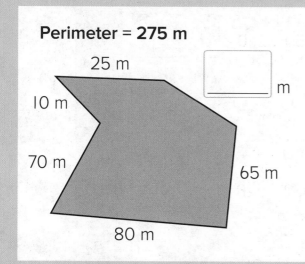

_____ m

25 m

10 m

70 m

65 m

80 m

This shape has been made by joining two rectangles.
Calculate the length of the unknown sides.

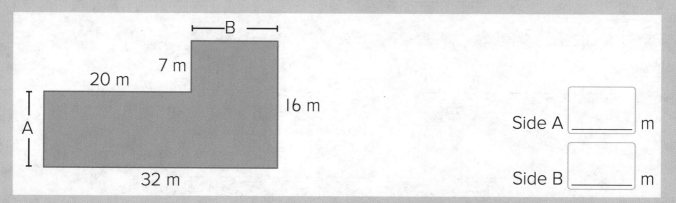

B

7 m

20 m

16 m

A

32 m

Side A _____ m

Side B _____ m

© ORIGO Education

© ORIGO Education

## Computation Practice — When is it unlucky to be followed by a black cat?

★ Complete the equations. Write each letter above its matching answer at the bottom of the page.

150 + 28 = ☐ **e**          308 + 39 = ☐ **a**

353 − 47 = ☐ **o**          230 − 55 = ☐ **e**

37 + 153 = ☐ **h**          58 + 234 = ☐ **e**

190 − 63 = ☐ **y**          450 − 240 = ☐ **o**

337 + 49 = ☐ **a**          126 + 37 = ☐ **w**

354 − 349 = ☐ **u**          532 − 528 = ☐ **u**

49 + 237 = ☐ **n**          62 + 317 = ☐ **r**

460 − 79 = ☐ **s**          340 − 65 = ☐ **m**

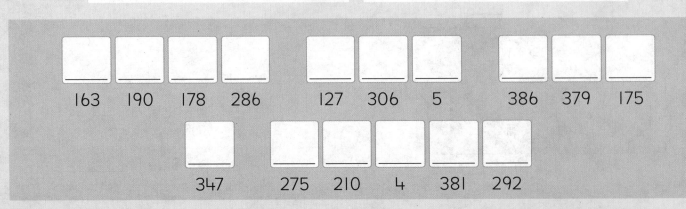

| | | | | | | | | | |
|---|---|---|---|---|---|---|---|---|---|
| 163 | 190 | 178 | 286 | 127 | 306 | 5 | 386 | 379 | 175 |

| | | | | | |
|---|---|---|---|---|---|
| 347 | 275 | 210 | 4 | 381 | 292 |

*ORIGO Stepping Stones* · Grade 3 · 12.10

1. Solve each problem. Show your thinking.

**a.** Abigail mixes 6 cups of water and 2 cups of lime juice for a party. How many 1-quart pitchers will she need to hold all the liquid?

 pitchers

**b.** Andre buys three 1-gallon containers of milk and four 1-pint cartons of juice. How many pints of liquid did he buy?

 pints

FROM 3.11.12

2. Calculate the length of the unknown side. Show your thinking.

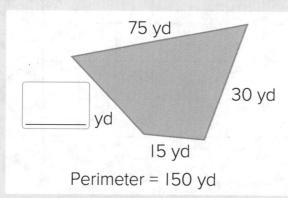

75 yd

30 yd

_____ yd

15 yd

Perimeter = 150 yd

FROM 3.12.10

## Preparing for Next Year

Complete each diagram.

**a.**

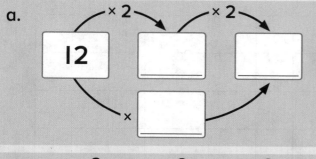

12

**b.**

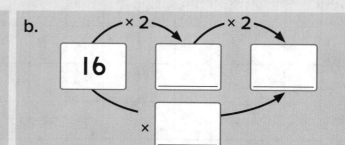

16

**c.**

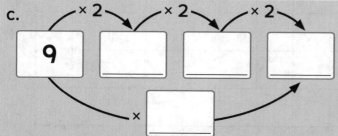

9

**d.**

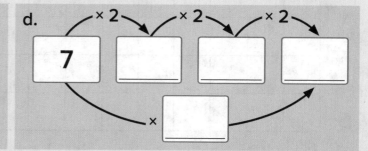

7

**Step In**   **What does the perimeter of a shape tell you?**

What does the area of a shape tell you?

How do you calculate perimeter? How do you calculate area?

What could be the dimensions of a rectangle with an area of 12 sq cm?

**Draw 3 different rectangles that each have an area of 12 sq cm and label the dimensions.**

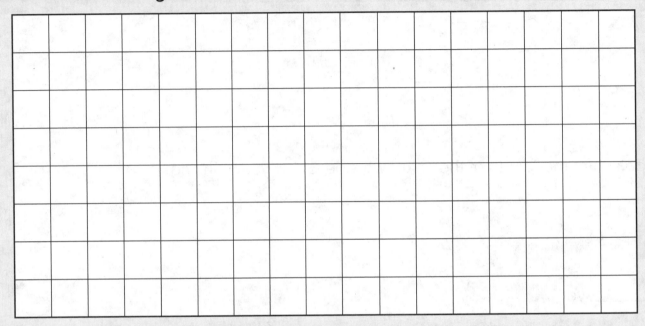

What do you notice about the perimeter of each shape?

**Step Up**   **1.  a.** Draw three different rectangles that each have an area of 16 sq cm. Label the rectangles **A**, **B**, and **C**.

**b.** Use the rectangles you drew in Question 1a on page 464 to complete this table.

| Rectangle | Length (cm) | Width (cm) | Perimeter (cm) | Area (sq cm) |
|---|---|---|---|---|
| A | | | | 16 |
| B | | | | 16 |
| C | | | | 16 |

**2. a.** Draw three different rectangles that each have a perimeter of 20 cm. Label the rectangles **D**, **E**, and **F**.

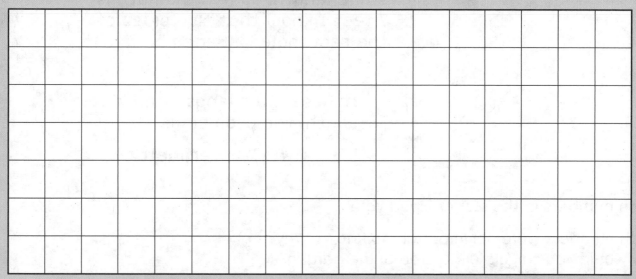

**b.** Use the rectangles you drew above to complete this table.

| Rectangle | Length (cm) | Width (cm) | Perimeter (cm) | Area (sq cm) |
|---|---|---|---|---|
| D | | | 20 | |
| E | | | 20 | |
| F | | | 20 | |

**Step Ahead**    Solve this problem. Show your thinking on page 470.

Naomi is building a sandbox. She wants the sandbox to have the greatest possible area. Naomi has 40 feet of lumber that she can cut to make the sides. What are the dimensions of the sandbox?

Length _____ ft

Width _____ ft

**Step In**

Luis is making edges for a rectangular garden. He wants to plant 5 rows of carrots. The dimensions of the garden are **6 feet by 7 feet**.

What is the perimeter of the garden?

What picture can you draw to match the story?

When I see the dimensions for a rectangle I need to remember that opposite sides will be the same length. So if the length is 7 feet I know that **two sides** of the rectangle will each be 7 feet.

If I use L for length and W for width, the problem is

**L + L + W + W = perimeter.**

**Which numbers in the story helped you?**

Which numbers were not important to know? Why?
How would you calculate the area of the garden?

**Step Up**

1. Draw a simple picture to match each story. Label the dimensions on your picture. Then write the answer.

**a.** Cole walked around the outside of a rectangular playground with 3 friends. Two sides are each 16 meters and two sides are each 7 meters. How far did Cole walk?

[_____] m

**b.** Carrina has a rectangular garden. Each long side measures 6 yards. Each short side is half the length. What is the area of the garden?

[_____] sq yd

**2.** Solve each problem. Show your thinking. Remember to show the correct units.

**a.** Donna has 6 square tiles. The perimeter of each tile is 20 inches. What is the area of each tile?

**b.** The perimeter of a rectangular barnyard is 64 meters. Each long side measures 19 meters. What is the length of each short side?

**c.** The perimeter of a triangle is 45 inches. One side is 17 inches long. The other sides are the same length. How long is each other side?

**d.** Isaac cuts out a rectangle that has a perimeter of 24 inches. The short side is 5 inches long. What is the area of the rectangle?

**Step Ahead**

The perimeter of a rectangle is 48 yards. The area of the same rectangle is greater than 100 square yards.

Draw a picture to figure out the possible dimensions.

Length is _____ yd

Width is _____ yd

## Think and Solve

Wendell can move two shapes to make the number of kilograms on each scale the same.

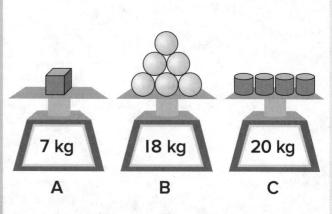

**a.** Which shapes can he move?

_____

**b.** Where can he move them?

_____

**c.** How many kilograms will be on each scale after the move? _____ kg

## Words at Work

Choose and write words from the list to complete these sentences. Some words are not used.

**a.** When three or more _____ meet, they make a _____ .

**b.** The _____ of a shape is the total distance around the shape.

**c.** To calculate the area of a rectangle, its _____ is multiplied by its width.

**d.** A _____ is a 3D object that has two identical faces joined together by _____ .

| Word list |
| --- |
| vertex |
| rectangles |
| base |
| perimeter |
| pyramid |
| length |
| area |
| edges |
| prism |

**1. a.** Three students threw paper airplanes. For each, write the distance of the flight or color the bar graph to show the result.

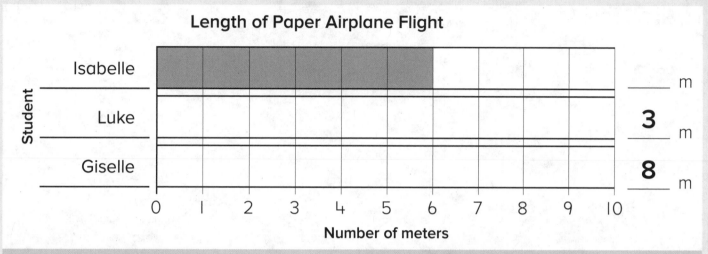

**Length of Paper Airplane Flight**

Isabelle _____ m

Luke **3** m

Giselle **8** m

**b.** Who threw their plane the farthest? _____

**c.** How many meters did Isabelle's airplane fly? _____ m

**2.** Solve each problem. Show your thinking.

**a.** A barnyard has 6 equal sides. The fence on each side is 15 feet long and 5 feet high. What is the perimeter of the barnyard?

_____ ft

**b.** The border of a rectangular garden is 36 meters. Each short side is 4 meters long. What is the length of each long side?

_____ m

Complete these equations.

**a.**
$40 = $ _____ $\times 10$

**b.**
_____ $\times 10 = 0$

**c.**
$10 \times$ _____ $= 80$

FROM 2.9.11

FROM 3.12.12

# STUDENT GLOSSARY

## Algorithm

**Algorithms** are rules used for completing tasks or for solving problems. There are standard algorithms for calculating answers to addition, subtraction, multiplication and division problems. This example shows the addition algorithm.

| H | T | O |
|---|---|---|
| 1 |   |   |
|   | 9 | 2 |
| + | 3 | 6 |
| 1 | 2 | 8 |

## Area

**Area** is the amount of surface that a shape covers. This amount is usually described in square units such as square centimeters (sq cm) or square inches (sq in).

## Capacity

**Capacity** is the amount something can hold.
A **gallon** is a customary unit of capacity. The short way to write gallon is **gal**.
A **liter** is a metric unit of capacity. The short way to write liter is **L**.
A **pint** is a unit of capacity. There are 2 pints in one quart.
The short way to write pint is **pt**.
A **quart** is a unit of capacity. There are 4 quarts in one gallon.
The short way to write quart is **qt**.

## Common Fraction

$\frac{2}{3}$ is shaded

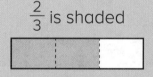

**Common fractions** describe equal parts of a whole. In this common fraction, 2 is the numerator and 3 is the denominator.

The **denominator** shows the number of equal parts (3) in the whole.
The **numerator** shows the number of those parts (2).

**Unit fractions** are common fractions that have a numerator of 1.

**Proper fractions** are common fractions that have a numerator that is less than the denominator. For example, $\frac{2}{5}$ is a proper fraction.

**Improper fractions** are common fractions that have a numerator that is greater than or equal to the denominator. For example, $\frac{7}{5}$ and $\frac{4}{4}$ are improper fractions.

**Equivalent fractions** are fractions that cover the same amount of area on a shape or are located on the same point on a number line.
For example: $\frac{1}{2}$ is equivalent to $\frac{2}{4}$

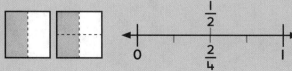

© ORIGO Education

# STUDENT GLOSSARY

## Comparing

When read from left to right, the symbol > means **is greater than**.
The symbol < means **is less than**.
For example:  2 < 6 **means** 2 is less than 6

## Division

**Division** is finding the number of equal groups or the number in each equal group when the total and one of these is known. For example, $8 \div \_\_ = 4$ or $8 \div 2 = \_\_$. This is recorded in a division equation that uses words or the $\div$ symbol. The result of division is called the **quotient**.

## Expanded form

A method of writing numbers as the sum of the values of each digit.
For example: $4,912 = (4 \times 1,000) + (9 \times 100) + (1 \times 10) + (2 \times 1)$

## Fact family

A multiplication **fact family** includes a multiplication fact, its turnaround fact, and the two related division facts.
For example:

$$4 \times 2 = 8$$
$$2 \times 4 = 8$$
$$8 \div 4 = 2$$
$$8 \div 2 = 4$$

## Length

**Length** is the measure of how long something is.

A **centimeter** is a metric unit of length. The short way to write centimeter is **cm**.

A **meter** is a metric unit of length. The short way to write meter is **m.**

## Line plot

A **line plot** is used to show data.
On this line plot, each dot represents one student.

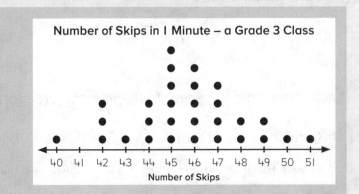

Number of Skips in 1 Minute – a Grade 3 Class

Number of Skips

## Mass

**Mass** is the amount something weighs.

A **gram** is a metric unit of mass. There are 1,000 grams in one kilogram.

The short way to write gram is **g**.

A **kilogram** is a metric unit of mass. The short way to write kilogram is **kg**.

## Mental computation strategies for multiplication

Strategies you can use to figure out a mathematical problem in your head.

### Use ten
*See* 5 × 7 *think* half of 10 × 7

### Doubling
*See* 2 × 7 *think* double 7
*See* 2 × 14 *think* double 14
*See* 4 × 7 *think* double, double 7
*See* 4 × 15 *think* double, double 15
*See* 8 × 7 *think* double, double, double 7
*See* 8 × 16 *think* double, double, double 16

### Double and halve (associative property)
*See* 6 × 35 *think* double 3 × 70

### Partial products (distributive property)
*See* 3 × 45 *think* (3 × 40) + (3 × 5)

### Use a known fact
*See* 6 × 8 *think* 5 × 8 + 8
*See* 3 × 9 *think* 3 × 10 − 3

## Mental computation strategies for division

**Halving** *See* 32 ÷ 4 *think* half of 32 is 16, half of 16 is 8

**Think multiplication** *See* 30 ÷ 5 *think* 5 × 6 = 30, so 30 ÷ 5 = 6

# STUDENT GLOSSARY

## Multiplication

**Multiplication** is finding the total when the number of equal groups or rows and the number in each group or row are known. This is recorded in a multiplication equation that uses the × symbol. The result of multiplication is called the **product**.

## Perimeter

A **perimeter** is the boundary of a shape and the total length of that boundary. For example, the perimeter of this rectangle is 20 inches.

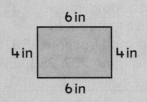

## Order of operations

If there is **one** type of operation in a sentence, work left to right.
If there is **more than one** type of operation, work left to right in this **order**:

**1.** Perform any operation inside parentheses.

**2.** Multiply or divide pairs of numbers.

**3.** Add or subtract pairs of numbers.

## Polyhedron

A **polyhedron** is any closed 3D object that has four or more flat faces.

When two surfaces meet, they make an **edge**.
When three or more edges meet, they make a **vertex**.

A **prism** is a polyhedron that has two identical faces that are joined by square or non-square rectangles. For example:

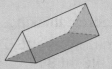

A **pyramid** is a polyhedron that has any polygon for a base. All the other faces joined to the base are triangles that meet at a point. For example:

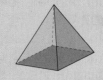

## Quadrilateral

A **quadrilateral** is any polygon (closed 2D shape) that has 4 straight sides.

Any quadrilateral that has all corners the same in size is called a **rectangle**.
Any quadrilateral that has all side the same in length is called a **rhombus**.

# TEACHER INDEX

# TEACHER INDEX

# TEACHER INDEX